FOCUS ON

Declarer Play

Master Point Press
22 Lower Village Gate
Toronto, ON
M5P 3L7
(416) 932-9766

Distributors:

In Canada: Hushion House 1-800-263-4374
In U.S.A.: APG 1-800-749-3292

Canadian Cataloguing In Publication Data
Roth, D.L.M. (Danny L.M.)
Focus on Declarer Play
ISBN 0-9698461-3-4
1. Contract Bridge — Dummy Play I. Title
GV1282.435.R68 1997   795.41'53   C97–931618-9

Cover and interior design: Zena Denchik
Editor: Ray Lee
Additional Analysis: Colin Lee

Printed and bound in Canada
1 2 3 4 5 6 7   03 02 01 00 99 98 97

FOCUS ON

Declarer Play

D A N N Y   R O T H

MASTER POINT PRESS

Contents

Foreword

Are you one of those players whose partners continually hog the bidding? Perhaps there's a reason — your declarer play! The most common mistakes made in this area can be summarised under three headings:

Poor use of options

Many declarers fail to realise that a hand may offer several chances of making a contract. All too often, they go for one specific line and then complain bitterly when the appropriate suit splits badly and/or a finesse fails. They then proceed to the next hand blissfully unaware that another, more successful line was available. The top-class declarer is continually on the look-out for ways to combine available chances to maximise his overall percentage of success.

Mishandling of communications

Many declarers underestimate the importance of communications between their own hand and dummy's, not to mention the possibly greater consideration of making life in this area difficult, if not impossible, for the defenders! An alarming number of players are simply unaware that it can even be worth sacrificing a trick to ensure good communications. The trick will usually be returned with interest.

Errors involving ruffing

The trump element is a complex factor in the game and is very often poorly understood. The purposes, uses and misuses of ruffing need to be studied in detail in the many situations in which there is scope for error. We shall start with some basics but then learn that knowledge in this area has to be handled with discretion. That is where the trouble arises.

Choosing the Best Line

1

Playing the Odds

Here we shall look at various suit combinations, first considering them in isolation and then understanding to what extent, if at all, our knowledge applies in the context of a whole hand.

Gravity precedes the coin toss!

Play for the drop before taking a finesse.

This position often arises in no-trump contracts where there are two long suits as possible sources for tricks. We shall start with this simple example:

W	N	E	S
Dealer South			
Neither vulnerable			
			1♣
pass	1♦	pass	1NT
pass	3NT		

North
♠ A Q 10 2
♥ J 5
♦ K 5 4 2
♣ K 8 3

South
♠ J 9 3
♥ A 6
♦ A 7 3
♣ A J 10 9 7

West leads the ♥4. You try the ♥J from dummy but East produces the ♥K. How do you play?

It is of little relevance whether you win the first or second round of hearts; the question is: 'What then?' You have three top tricks in the red suits and thus six more are required. Two approaches are possible:

hope to find the ♣Q to bring in five clubs and one spade, or hope for a successful finesse against the ♠K to pick up four spades and two top clubs. How do you combine the chances? Looking at the clubs alone, it is a better chance to play one top card and then finesse against the queen (about 53%) rather than to play for the drop (about 30%). But these figures consider the club suit in isolation. Playing for the drop entitles you to hold the lead, after which you still have a 50% chance in spades. If you finesse clubs unsuccessfully, four quick heart tricks will defeat you immediately. Thus playing for the drop first (in clubs) followed by a finesse in spades will give you a (30 + 0.5 x 70) = about a 65% chance for the contract. This is, therefore, the best line.

North
♠ A Q 10 2
♥ J 5
♦ K 5 4 2
♣ K 8 3

West
♠ 8 7
♥ Q 10 8 4 2
♦ J 9 8 6
♣ Q 2

East
♠ K 6 5 4
♥ K 9 7 3
♦ Q 10
♣ 6 5 4

South
♠ J 9 3
♥ A 6
♦ A 7 3
♣ A J 10 9 7

Points to remember

1. Playing for the drop wins over an immediate finesse in the important respect of enabling you to hold the lead.
2. Note how the technique of combining chances increases the overall chance of making the contract markedly. This is worthwhile, even at pairs, taking into account the risk of conceding an extra undertrick.

Be the greediest pig in the sty!

Do not ignore those little extra chances — plan your play to take advantage of them.

Many players take the view that the odd one per cent or so

matters little. Over the short term, they are probably right but, in the long run, cents add up to dollars or, depending where you are, pence add up to pounds:

Dealer South				**North**
Neither vulnerable				♠ A Q 10 4 2
W	**N**	**E**	**S**	♥ Q 9 4 2
			1♣	♦ 6 3
pass	1♠	pass	2NT	♣ 10 2
pass	3♥	pass	3NT	

South
♠ K 7
♥ 10 6 3
♦ K Q 4
♣ A K Q 6 4

West leads the ♦J to his partner's ♦A and East returns the ♦5. How do you play?

Well, which black suit do you prefer? In fact, spades offer the slightly better chance in that, with the ♠10 in the long hand, you will gain if the ♠J drops on the second round; this does not apply in clubs. But take no credit if you played on spades right away. It costs nothing to play one top club first to be able to take advantage of a singleton ♣J. If it does not appear, revert to spades. If they do not break, you will have to try the clubs, prepared to give up the fourth round. You will hope that the hand with the long club has both top heart honours and does not hold the ♠J. You may then get a diamond entry back to hand or two heart tricks and the fifth spade.

North
♠ A Q 10 4 2
♥ Q 9 4 2
♦ 6 3
♣ 10 2

West
♠ 8 6
♥ A 8
♦ J 10 8 2
♣ 9 8 7 5 3

East
♠ J 9 5 3
♥ K J 7 5
♦ A 9 7 5
♣ J

South
♠ K 7
♥ 10 6 3
♦ K Q 4
♣ A K Q 6 4

As the cards lie, your good technique will earn you four club tricks, two diamonds and three top spades.

Points to remember

1.   Note the difference between those two black suit holdings. The ♠K must be kept as an entry to the clubs in case the ♣J does fall singleton.
2.   Playing one round of clubs first can never cost in any circumstances.

A suit is one thing — the wardrobe is another!

We have seen already that the 'correct' play in a single suit is not necessarily correct in the context of the whole hand. This can be important in the area of communications:

Dealer North
N-S vulnerable

W	N	E	S
	1♦	pass	1♥
pass	2NT	pass	6♥

North
♠ K Q 4
♥ Q J
♦ A K Q 3 2
♣ 9 8 5

South
♠ A 5
♥ A K 5 4 3 2
♦ 6 4
♣ K 10 3

How do you play this hand on the lead of the ♠J?

It seems natural to win the first trick in hand to avoid blocking the suit, but try doing so and down you will go! Consideration of the whole hand, however, will guide you to the winning line. You must be prepared for the trumps to split 4-1. Then you will have to manage your entries carefully to take six trump tricks, using the honours separately, as well as three diamonds and three top spades.

Win the first spade in dummy, cash the ♥Q and ♥J, cross to the ♠A in hand and then draw trumps before claiming twelve tricks. Winning the first spade in hand leaves South without the sure entry needed to draw the trumps if a bad split makes it impractical to overtake one of dummy's heart honours. Of course, the ♣A might be onside, but why reduce a 100% contract to a 50% chance?

North
♠ K Q 4
♥ Q J
♦ A K Q 3 2
♣ 9 8 5

West
♠ J 10 9 7 3 2
♥ 9
♦ 9 8
♣ A Q J 4

East
♠ 8 6
♥ 10 8 7 6
♦ J 10 7 5
♣ 7 6 2

South
♠ A 5
♥ A K 5 4 3 2
♦ 6 4
♣ K 10 3

Points to remember

1. This is a classic illustration of the need to play through the whole hand mentally before touching a single card.

2. Note that, whereas, in most circumstances, entries to dummy's long suit should be a first priority, here we have a position where entries to hand to draw trumps take precedence.

Circumstances alter cases!

We now consider a hand where the degree of optimism in the bidding is crucial:

Dealer South
Neither vulnerable

W	N	E	S
			2♣
pass	2♦	pass	2NT
pass	3♦[1]	pass	3♥
pass	5♥[2]	pass	6♥

[1] transfer to ♥
[2] invitational, looking for controls and trump quality

North
♠ 9 5
♥ K Q J 9 8 5
♦ 7 5 4
♣ 10 3

South
♠ A 7 2
♥ A 10
♦ A K J 9 6
♣ A K J

How do you play on the lead of the ♠Q — and would it make any difference if the contract were 7♥?

In 6♥, you can have two bites at the cherry, but the shortage of resources in dummy implies that you have to be careful about entries. You should duck the first spade and win the second round. Now draw trumps and cash the two top diamonds and one top club. If either minor queen falls, the hand is over. If neither appears, cross to dummy with a spade ruff and try the club finesse. This is clearly a superior line to the straightforward 50% diamond finesse.

Sadly, when this hand occurred, the deal was:

North
♠ 9 5
♥ K Q J 9 8 5
♦ 7 5 4
♣ 10 3

West
♠ Q J 10 4 3
♥ 6 3
♦ 10 2
♣ Q 9 7 2

East
♠ K 8 6
♥ 7 4 2
♦ Q 8 3
♣ 8 6 5 4

South
♠ A 7 2
♥ A 10
♦ A K J 9 6
♣ A K J

Declarer played two top diamonds and duly went two down when the club finesse failed, leaving the ♦Q still to be lost. This declarer actually made three fewer tricks compared to other tables where the contract was an ambitious 7♥. In the grand slam, the diamonds must come in and you obviously cannot afford the spade duck. Win the first spade, cash the ♥A and one top diamond. Finish drawing trumps and take the diamond finesse to make the contract.

This hand illustrates how much injustice there can be in this game. On correct play, a sensible 6♥ goes two off while a speculative grand slam makes. Anyone for Bingo?

Points to remember

1. Note the importance of that spade duck to ensure communications. Try replaying the hand on the same line without it. ♠A, draw trumps, cash ♦A, ♦K, ♣A and play a spade. Now the defenders can win and cash the ♦Q before you have had a chance to try the club finesse.

Ducking the first round when you have A x x opposite x x in a suit contract is very often a good play, disrupting opponents' communications. It should usually only be rejected if you deem it dangerous to leave opponents on play (e.g. if a dangerous switch is threatened).

2.   Observe that the 'percentage' play is not necessarily a winning play on a specific hand. But while you are entitled to feel aggrieved on this occasion, you will win in the long term and that, after all, is what matters.

Long suits are there to be worn!

Now try a more complicated example:

Dealer North
Neither vulnerable

W	N	E	S
	1♦	pass	1♥
pass	2♣	pass	2♠¹
pass	3♣	pass	3♥
pass	4♥	pass	5♥²
pass	6♥		

¹ fourth-suit, game-forcing
² invitational, looking for
  trump quality and
  controls

North
♠ K
♥ A 7
♦ A J 5 4 2
♣ A 9 6 4 2

South
♠ A 8
♥ K J 10 9 5 3 2
♦ Q 10 7
♣ K

West leads the ♠J. How do you play?

First, count your tricks. Assuming one trump trick will be lost (no problem otherwise), there are six heart tricks, two top clubs, two top spades and the ♦A to total eleven, so that it appears that the diamond finesse will be needed.

But you should not ignore the extra chance of setting up a long club if the suit breaks 4-3. Win the first spade perforce in dummy, cash the ♣K, cross to the ♥A and ruff a club in hand. Now the key play — ruff the ♠A to gain an extra entry to dummy, before ruffing a further club! Now the ♥K reveals the poor trump split but, after conceding a trump trick, the two losing diamonds in hand can be discarded on the two good clubs in dummy if everyone has followed to three rounds of the suit.

North
♠ K
♥ A 7
♦ A J 5 4 2
♣ A 9 6 4 2

West
♠ J 10 6 5 3 2
♥ 6
♦ 8 6
♣ Q 10 8 5

East
♠ Q 9 7 4
♥ Q 8 4
♦ K 9 3
♣ J 7 3

South
♠ A 8
♥ K J 10 9 5 3 2
♦ Q 10 7
♣ K

Points to remember

1. Note the technique of trying to establish the clubs by ruffing before attempting the diamond finesse.

2. An initial diamond lead would have made life more difficult and now the best line is more debatable. Given that he now has an extra entry in spades, South could try a similar approach: ♦A, refusing the finesse, ♣K, ♠K, ♣A discarding a diamond, club ruffed in hand, ♥A, fourth club ruffed with an intermediate trump and, if that goes through uninterrupted (i.e. West has four clubs or three clubs but not the ♥Q), ♠A ruffed in dummy and the fifth club, discarding the last losing diamond to concede one trump trick as before. Alternatively, South may finesse the diamond at trick one and hope to guess the trump position correctly if the ♦K has to be lost.

3. Note the key play of ruffing of a winning spade to gain the extra entry to dummy. That spade ace has no value!

Pitch first then putt!

The principle of drop first, then finesse, which we discussed in earlier hands, can be extended to positions where a loser needs to be discarded early. Calculation of percentages may be relevant:

Dealer South
Neither vulnerable

W	N	E	S
			2♠[1]
pass	4NT	pass	5♣
pass	6♠		

[1] weak two bid

North
♠ K 9 7 5
♥ A 7
♦ A 2
♣ A K Q 4 2

South
♠ Q J 10 4 3 2
♥ K J 2
♦ 7 5
♣ 8 6

West leads the ♦K. How do you play the hand?

Clearly you have to win the first trick and discard your diamond loser before touching trumps. There are two possibilities: bang down three top clubs or try the heart finesse. On the face of it, the heart finesse offers the better chance at slightly less than 50% (as both defenders will have to follow three times unless the short hand has a trump void or the bare ace) as against the 3-3 club break at 36%. So did you back the odds? In fact, the club line is slightly superior. It will work whenever the clubs are 3-3 (36%) and, in half the cases where they are 4-2 (24%) East will have the shortage and will ruff the third round. You can overruff and still have the chance to try your luck in hearts. So that already gives you an extra 12%. In addition, the hand with the short clubs could be forced to ruff with a single-ton ace of trumps or have no trumps at all. That swings the odds in favour of playing on clubs.

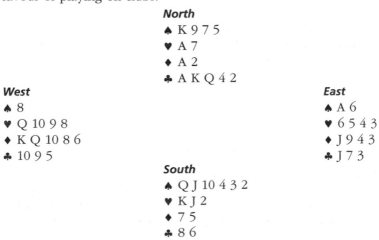

North
♠ K 9 7 5
♥ A 7
♦ A 2
♣ A K Q 4 2

West
♠ 8
♥ Q 10 9 8
♦ K Q 10 8 6
♣ 10 9 5

East
♠ A 6
♥ 6 5 4 3
♦ J 9 4 3
♣ J 7 3

South
♠ Q J 10 4 3 2
♥ K J 2
♦ 7 5
♣ 8 6

Points to remember

1. The percentage difference between the two lines may be small but little things add up over the years. The important point is to realise that playing on clubs gives far more chances than simply a 3-3 break.
2. On a non-diamond lead, there is time to draw trumps.

We shall now turn to positions where an option may only exist in one area but not in another.

Take Hobson's choice first!

Where you have two suits and, in one, there is no choice of how to play while, in another, there is, attack the 'no-choice' suit first. What happens may influence the way you play the second suit.

This kind of consideration arises when a safety play is available and it is a question of whether or not declarer can afford it. Here is a model example:

Dealer West   **North**
Both vulnerable   ♠ 9 5 4

W	N	E	S	
pass	1♣	pass	1♥	
pass	2♥	pass	6♥	

North
♠ 9 5 4
♥ Q 8 4 3
♦ K Q 6
♣ A J 2

South
♠ A Q J
♥ A 10 7 6 5 2
♦ A J 10
♣ 8

West leads the ♣K. How do you play the trumps?

The answer is simple — you do not! The spade finesse cannot be avoided so it should be taken first. If it succeeds, then you simply have to avoid two trump losers and a safety play is in order. There is no problem if the trumps are 2-1 but if they are all in one hand, banging down the ace would spell disaster if East has all three trumps, while starting with the queen would lose to West's ♥K J 9. The correct line is to start with a low heart from dummy. If East follows low, put in the ten. If that loses, the suit has broken 2-1. If East fails to follow, rise with the ace and play a low card through West. The initial play of a low card towards the queen is also likely to be good enough but is inferior as it costs the overtrick if East has a singleton king. It also very slightly increases the risk as there may be an enemy ruff.

If the spade finesse fails, a safety play in trumps is obviously out of the question. You could either run the ♥Q, hoping to find East with ♥K 9 and West with a singleton ♥J or, twice as good a chance, bang down the ace, hoping for a singleton king either side.

North
♠ 9 5 4
♥ Q 8 4 3
♦ K Q 6
♣ A J 2

West
♠ 10 8 3
♥ —
♦ 9 8 5 2
♣ K Q 6 5 4 3

East
♠ K 7 6 2
♥ K J 9
♦ 7 4 3
♣ 10 9 7

South
♠ A Q J
♥ A 10 7 6 5 2
♦ A J 10
♣ 8

Points to remember

1. Note again declarer's refusal to commit himself to a critical play until the last possible moment.
2. A knowledge of suit combinations (at least the common ones) and how to play them for a specified number of tricks is a vital piece of the expert's armoury.

2

Guessing Right

It is a common belief, both in life and in bridge, that some people are luckier than others. In this chapter, we shall learn that a good player can make, or at least increase, his own luck. As we have already seen, when guesswork is involved, the winning declarer refuses to commit himself until he has gathered as much information as possible.

Wait for daylight!

Make no decision without full information! All too often, declarers rush into a specific line of play when it is unnecessary to commit themselves. It amounts to groping in the dark for no reason. It costs so little to switch on the light first. This is a typical hand on which many players would throw a fortune out of the window.

Dealer East				**North**
Neither vulnerable				♠ K J 8 2
W	**N**	**E**	**S**	♥ K Q
		pass	2NT	♦ A 9 5 4
pass	7NT			♣ A 8 3

South
♠ A Q 9 4
♥ A 5
♦ K Q 10 2
♣ K Q J

West leads the ♥6. How do you play the diamonds?

The answer is very simple — you don't! If they are 3-2, there is no problem. Even if the ♦J heads a 4-card suit you can pick him up on either side, but you have to guess which hand to lead the suit from. The solution to this dilemma is to play other suits off first. Now, if one defender proves to be short in both black suits, having started, say, with one spade and two clubs, he can hardly have a singleton diamond as that would leave him with nine hearts and, if both defenders follow to two hearts, even that is ruled out. Thus you should cash the ♦K and win the second round in the hand that can lead through the defender likely to be long in diamonds.

In another case, for example, suppose West follows to three spades and East follows to only two clubs while both follow to two hearts. East has shown two clubs, two hearts, and two spades against West's five clubs, two hearts and three spades. West cannot have more than three diamonds; thus you must be prepared for East to have the possible diamond length.

In a less clear-cut case, where West shows three spades, three clubs, and two hearts, while East shows two spades, three clubs, and three hearts (discarding a third heart on the third round of spades), no play is certain, but, assuming that West discards a club and East a heart on the fourth round of spades, East is the slight favourite to hold the long diamonds as you know that West had seven black cards to East's five and the red-suit situation is uncertain.

Points to remember

1.   Avoid taking a crucial decision until you have maximum information.
2.   But ensure that it is not too expensive to get that information. Here we had an extreme case where you could afford to cash every non-diamond trick in sight before committing yourself. Entry considerations, for example, may restrict you to a partial count.

At least eat the hors d'oeuvre!

Often a declarer has a great deal of information to work on before he starts to play the hand, as a result of the bidding. This is especially true when one of the opponents has shown a long suit by pre-empting, as counting out the defenders hands can become a very simple matter. Here is an example:

Dealer East   **North**
Both vulnerable   ♠ K J 4
| W | N | E | S | ♥ K 4
|---|---|---|---| ♦ K 9 5 4 3
| | | 3♥ | 3NT | ♣ A 9 8
| pass | 6NT | | |

South
♠ A Q 3
♥ A 6
♦ A J 10 6
♣ K 5 4 2

At this vulnerability, you may be confident that East holds at least a seven-card suit. West leads the ♥9. How do you play the diamonds?

Again, the answer is simple — you don't! With East having pre-empted, West is hot favourite to hold the ♦Q but why commit yourself now when you do not have to? Try a couple of rounds of spades; you never know what might happen. Say you play one spade and East discards a heart. How do you play diamonds now?

Again, the answer is simple — you don't! If anything, the odds now have swung in favour of East's holding the ♦Q but why not find out more? Surely, three rounds of clubs will prove most enlightening. Duck the first or second round to maintain control, win the return and cash a high club. When the suit breaks 3-3, you know West started with two hearts, seven spades, and three clubs, and thus cannot have more than one diamond. With confidence, you cash the ♦K and take a marked finesse through East.

North
♠ K J 4
♥ K 4
♦ K 9 5 4 3
♣ A 9 8

West   **East**
♠ 10 9 8 7 6 5 2   ♠ —
♥ 9 5   ♥ Q J 10 8 7 3 2
♦ 7   ♦ Q 8 2
♣ J 10 6   ♣ Q 7 3

South
♠ A Q 3
♥ A 6
♦ A J 10 6
♣ K 5 4 2

Points to remember

1. Note the duck of an early club; this ensures that you can play the requisite number of rounds to complete the count without losing control.
2. Get into the habit of counting hands as often as possible. Yes, it is a strain, but the dividends are enormous. Here you have turned a 50% slam into a certainty — that adds up over time.
3. A small but significant matter — notice the advantage of this contract over 6♦. In the suit slam, you would have had to draw trumps at once for fear of a ruff and, ignorant of the spade position, would very probably have gone wrong. There are no ruffing values in this hand and therefore, with a double stopper in hearts, nothing to gain by having a trump suit. On top of this, of course, 6NT scores better in pairs' events.

Her Majesty regrets!

We shall now consider a hand which combines the above principle with that of the play in a single suit having to be considered in the context of the whole hand:

Dealer East   **North**
Both vulnerable   ♠ K J 2
                                      ♥ K Q 3
| W | N | E | S | ♦ A 5
|---|---|---|---| ♣ A J 8 5 3
| | | pass | 2NT |
| pass | 7NT | | |
                                      South
                                      ♠ A Q 10
                                      ♥ A J 10
                                      ♦ K Q J
                                      ♣ K 10 4 2

West leads the ♠9, East following with the ♠5. Plan the play

Despite the 38 points combined, the ♣Q still has to be located; how should you play the club suit? The correct approach is to consider that, if the suit breaks 2-2 or 3-1, it is a pure guess as to where you seek the lady but, if they are 4-0, then only a stack with West can be picked up. It is, therefore, correct to start with the ♣K and then take a decision if both opponents follow and West plays low on the second round. But that is considering the club suit in isolation! Take no credit unless you cashed some side-suit winners first. In fact, East shows out on the second spade and all follow to the six red-suit winners. So West has shown six spades and at least six red cards, leaving him with, at most, one club. If he is void, the contract is doomed. You must hope he has a singleton and play low to the ♣A, intending to take the marked finesse through East on the way back.

North
♠ K J 2
♥ K Q 3
♦ A 5
♣ A J 8 5 3

West
♠ 9 8 7 6 4 3
♥ 7 5 2
♦ 10 8 3
♣ 7

East
♠ 5
♥ 9 8 6 4
♦ 9 7 6 4 2
♣ Q 9 6

South
♠ A Q 10
♥ A J 10
♦ K Q J
♣ K 10 4 2

Points to remember
1. Note that this contract is superior to 7♣ on two counts. Firstly, there is nothing to be gained from North's ruffing value and that, in the suit contract, a decision has to be made on the clubs before the other suits can be tested. A good technician would now probably go down.
2. It is instructive to note that, if everybody follows to the side-suit winners and the absolute count is therefore unclear, the odds in favour of a 2-2 club split have increased markedly from their original, or *a priori* 40%.

Reap in the full harvest!

Bridge encyclopedias show pages of suit combinations and how to play them. Learning these is extremely tedious work and, worse still, can be counterproductive. Some knowledge in this area, is, however, essential. Suit combinations should be played to best advantage.

While it is very difficult to memorise every possible suit combination and space does not permit us to cover every one, the following are illustrative examples in which even fairly good players continually go wrong:

Dealer East
N-S vulnerable

W	N	E	S
		pass	1♣
pass	1♦	pass	2♣
pass	2♥	pass	2NT
pass	3NT		

North
♠ A 6 3 2
♥ A K 9 7
♦ A 10 9 7
♣ 5

South
♠ K 10 8
♥ 6 2
♦ K 5
♣ A J 8 7 6 4

West leads the ♥Q and you win in dummy, East playing the ♥3. On the ♣5, East plays the ♣K. How do you play?

The clubs will have to be brought in and you must set up the suit while losing only two tricks in it, otherwise you will lack sufficient entries. If the suit splits 3-3, there is no problem and you will succeed, regardless of how you tackle the suit. If it splits 4-2, your choice is critical. After winning the first round with the ace, to which West follows with the ♣3, playing a small card may win against a (now) singleton ♣Q while playing the ♣J succeeds against either a (now) singleton ♣10 or ♣9, twice as likely. Therefore it is right to play the ♣J on the second round.

North
♠ A 6 3 2
♥ A K 9 7
♦ A 10 9 7
♣ 5

West
♠ Q 9 7 4
♥ Q J 10 8
♦ 4 3 2
♣ 10 3

East
♠ J 5
♥ 5 4 3
♦ Q J 8 6
♣ K Q 9 2

South
♠ K 10 8
♥ 6 2
♦ K 5
♣ A J 8 7 6 4

Points to remember

1. In suit combination problems of this type, mentally run through the possible enemy distributions and consider those in which your play is critical.

2. In those cases, choose the play which gives you the highest probability of success, accepting that you cannot be right all the time. In the above example you would lose out had East had ♣ K Q doubleton, but it is better to look silly once than twice!

Study the variations on a theme!

Having seen the idea, try this next example; again, the king and queen in the critical suit are in the defenders' hands:

Dealer East				**North**
N-S vulnerable				♠ A 6 3 2
W	**N**	**E**	**S**	♥ A K 9 7
		pass	1♣	♦ A 10 9 7
pass	1♦	pass	2♣	♣ 5
pass	2♥	pass	2NT	
pass	3NT			**South**
				♠ K 10 8
				♥ 6 2
				♦ K 5
				♣ A J 10 7 6 4

Again, the lead of the ♥Q is won in dummy. Now, on the ♣5, East plays the ♣2. How do you play?

Too many players would finesse the ♣10 without a second thought. Again, a 3-3 break will see you home in all cases, so if the cards lie in that friendly a fashion, you can play the suit in any reasonably sensible manner you care to. Admittedly, too, a finesse will gain overtricks when East has exactly ♣ K Q x. However, even at match points, making this contract is likely more important than whether you can make overtricks. You must consider the 4-2 splits, which are more likely than the 3-3 divisions; the finesse gains where East has exactly ♣ K Q x x but the ♣A followed by a low card gains where either defender has a doubleton honour — far more likely. Your percentage play is therefore to win the ♣A and play a low club off the dummy.

North
♠ A 6 3 2
♥ A K 9 7
♦ A 10 9 7
♣ 5

West
♠ Q 9 7 4
♥ Q J 10 8
♦ 4 3 2
♣ K 3

East
♠ J 5
♥ 5 4 3
♦ Q J 8 6
♣ Q 9 8 2

South
♠ K 10 8
♥ 6 2
♦ K 5
♣ A J 10 7 6 4

Note that leading the ♣J or ♣10 on the second round of clubs achieves nothing in the 3-3 cases and loses an unnecessary trick and the contract when a defender has a doubleton honour.

Points to remember

1. The recommended play applied because you could afford to lose two tricks in the club suit. Had the situation required you to bring in five club tricks, the finesse would be correct as you must hope for East to hold exactly ♣ K Q x.

2. Still discussing the case where five tricks are required, consider the position where the bidding marks most or all of the outstanding high cards with West. The correct play now would be the ♣A followed by a low card. The only hope is to find ♣K Q doubleton to your left.

3. Notice, therefore, how the case of a particular hand can throw the 'percentage' fanatic right out and how vital it is to understand what you are doing rather than playing, parrot fashion, on the basis of "The 'expert' said. . ."

Cutting their cables!

We now consider declarer's play when a long suit is led against him at no-trumps. A remarkable number of players would go wrong on the following hand.

Dealer South
Neither vulnerable

W	N	E	S
			1♣
pass	1♦	pass	1NT
pass	3NT		

North
♠ A 8 7
♥ Q J 6 3
♦ K J 4 2
♣ K 10

South
♠ Q J 3
♥ A K 5
♦ 7 3
♣ Q J 9 8 2

West leads the ♦6. How do you play? In particular, which card do you play on trick one?

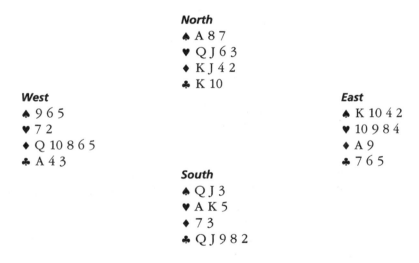

North
♠ A 8 7
♥ Q J 6 3
♦ K J 4 2
♣ K 10

West
♠ 9 6 5
♥ 7 2
♦ Q 10 8 6 5
♣ A 4 3

East
♠ K 10 4 2
♥ 10 9 8 4
♦ A 9
♣ 7 6 5

South
♠ Q J 3
♥ A K 5
♦ 7 3
♣ Q J 9 8 2

At the time, declarer tried the ♦J and went down when the deal was as above. There was no rush; any diamond finesse can wait. Just play low and let East win — he cannot now hurt you.

Points to remember

1. Note the play of a low card from dummy's diamond holding; the tenace is kept intact and East can hardly attack it profitably.
2. With the first trick lost to the ♦9, the suit is now hopelessly blocked.

From a jack to a king!

We shall now consider another position where declarer holds the king and the jack in the enemy suit and may need to commit himself at the first trick. Here a 'guess' is involved — or is it?

Dealer North				**North**
N-S vulnerable				♠ 7 6 5

W	**N**	**E**	**S**	
	pass	pass	2NT	♥ K 7 3
pass	3NT			♦ J 9 7 5

♣ J 8 4

South
♠ A J
♥ J 6 5
♦ A K Q
♣ K Q 10 6 3

West leads the ♥2. How do you play the hand?

Assuming West's lead is fourth best, it is clear that, if you play low on the first heart, you are guaranteed a trick in the suit whilst putting up the king risks losing four tricks immediately followed by the ♣A. The best approach is to consider the four possible arrangements of the enemy heart honours in turn:

a) If West has both ♥A and ♥Q, playing low will net two tricks in the suit; but playing the ♥K will not cost the contract as you will lose only three heart tricks and the ♣A.

b) If East has both ♥A and ♥Q, it matters little what you play. East will win and realise that, by persisting with the suit, he can only hope for three heart tricks and the ♣A. He will thus switch to spades to ensure success.

c) If West holds the ♥Q and East the ♥A, you appear to be better placed playing low at trick one but again, East should realise that there is no further hope in hearts and switch to spades. Thus, in this case, sound defence is likely to defeat you. You have no hope unless there is a 6-2 or wilder spade split and the ♣A is with the spade shortage.

d) If East holds the ♥Q and West holds the ♥A, it is now crucial to rise with the ♥K.

To sum up, you have no realistic chance if East has the ♥A and thus you should play West for it and rise with the ♥K. After knocking out the ♣A, you will concede three heart tricks but no more.

North
♠ 7 6 5
♥ K 7 3
♦ J 9 7 5
♣ J 8 4

West
♠ Q 10 4
♥ A 10 8 2
♦ 10 8 6 3
♣ 5 2

East
♠ K 9 8 3 2
♥ Q 9 4
♦ 4 2
♣ A 9 7

South
♠ A J
♥ J 6 5
♦ A K Q
♣ K Q 10 6 3

Points to remember

1. Note the way the various possibilities were worked out by declarer.
2. Observe that the defenders, on realising that the fourth-high lead limits the number of tricks available in hearts, will look elsewhere if given the chance. Thus, even at the risk of losing an 'unnecessary' trick, do not give them that chance.

Find the lady!

Now look at another example:

Dealer West
E-W vulnerable

W	N	E	S
2♥[1]	dbl	pass	3♥
pass	3NT	pass	4♠
pass	5♣	pass	5♦
pass	5♥	pass	6♠

[1] weak two-bid

North
♠ K Q 8 4
♥ A 7
♦ J 4
♣ A 10 6 3 2

South
♠ A J 10 9 3
♥ 9
♦ A Q 6
♣ K J 5 4

West leads the ♥K. How are you going to play the clubs?

Eight ever, nine never! is a rule taught to beginners and intermediate players when catching a missing queen is discussed. But the exceptions are so abundant that it is almost better not to know the rule. Can you find the lady here?

You win and draw trumps in two rounds. How do you play from here? Eventually, you are going to have to make a decision on the clubs. Do you consider that the 'eight ever, nine never' rule applies?

In situations where a queen is missing and you have the choice of finessing either way or playing for the drop, the best approach is to consider what happens if you make a choice and it proves to be wrong. In that event, will you be able to salvage something from the wreckage?

Following this logic, it is consideration of the position in the diamond suit that will lead you to the solution. Assume you first ruff a heart to eliminate that suit. Now let's look at all three possible lines of play in clubs:

a) *Play for the drop.*

This will win even if East shows out in the second round. A third round of clubs will put West on play and he will either have to give you a free finesse in diamonds or lead a third round of hearts to give you a ruff and discard. But if West shows out, your contract will be at the mercy of the diamond finesse.

b) *Cash the king and take a finesse through West.*

This will win if West has the ♣Q but, if East has her, doubleton or longer, again you will have to take the diamond finesse.

c) *Cash the ace and take a finesse through East.*

This is the winning line. If East shows out on the second round, you rise with the ♣K and lead a third round of clubs to put West in to lead a red suit and give you the contract. If East follows to the second round and West does prove to have the ♣Q, then clubs have broken 2-2 and now West is again endplayed, and forced to give you the contract with a red-card exit. If East has the ♣Q, however, the finesse will succeed and the contract only fails if he started with all four outstanding clubs (since you still have a club loser in that case) and the diamond finesse is also wrong.

North
♠ K Q 8 4
♥ A 7
♦ J 4
♣ A 10 6 3 2

West
♠ 7 3
♥ K Q 10 8 6 3
♦ K 10 8 2
♣ 7

East
♠ 6 5
♥ J 5 4 2
♦ 9 7 5 3
♣ Q 9 8

South
♠ A J 10 9 2
♥ 9
♦ A Q 6
♣ K J 5 4

Points to remember

1. Note the importance of drawing trumps and eliminating hearts before tackling clubs.
2. In all play decisions, noting whether you can recover if you choose the wrong option will often be the guide to the right line.

No ice — no dice!

Having seen the idea, try this next example. We all remember those immortal words from Marilyn Monroe!

Dealer West
E-W vulnerable

W	N	E	S
1♠	dbl	2♠	4♥

North
♠ A 6
♥ Q 10 9 6 4
♦ K 7 5
♣ A 6 3

South
♠ 8 7 3
♥ A 8 7 3 2
♦ A 6 2
♣ 5 4

Rather than give the impression of 'just competing', you have taken a flier to game on minimal values. What is your plan after the lead of the ♠K, East playing the ♠10?

The ♥K may drop, or you could run the ♥Q, hoping West has a singleton ♥J, but the probability is that you will lose a trick in each suit. Can anything be done if the trump loser cannot be avoided?

You will not be able to avoid the club or spade loser but you could have better luck in diamonds. Suppose you could arrange for the trump trick to be lost when the black suits have been eliminated and West, who is likely to have the ♥K on the bidding, is out of diamonds. You will have to assume that West has two diamonds and East five. To prepare the ground, duck the first spade, win the continuation (a diamond is best for the defence) and duck a club in both hands.

Win the next diamond, cash the black aces and cross to the trump ace, ruff your last spade and dummy's last club. Now exit in trumps.

North
♠ A 6
♥ Q 10 9 6 4
♦ K 7 5
♣ A 6 3

West
♠ K Q J 4 2
♥ K 5
♦ 9 4
♣ K Q 7 2

East
♠ 10 9 5
♥ J
♦ Q J 10 8 3
♣ J 10 9 8

South
♠ 8 7 3
♥ A 8 7 3 2
♦ A 6 2
♣ 5 4

In this fortunate layout, after ten tricks, you reach a position where West is on play, and, left with nothing but black cards, must give you a ruff and discard.

Points to remember

1. Note declarer's necessary assumption that West has two diamonds and East five. A 4-3 break would have been fatal.
2. Note East's play of the ♠10 under the ♠K after he had supported his partner. This is often done by a defender with a very weak hand to indicate a possible entry. Here the ten would indicate the nine and deny the jack.

3

Avoiding Finesses

One of the earliest techniques taught to beginners is the finesse. Once having learnt the craft, it is disheartening to find that the next lesson is 'how to avoid having to use it!' Beware, for example, of taking a finesse which can potentially create blockage in the suit, particularly when the finesse itself gains nothing.

Don't put your head on the block!

	North		
Dealer North	♠ A J 10 9 7		
E-W vulnerable	♥ 6		

W	N	E	S
	1♠	pass	2♥
pass	2♠	pass	3NT

♦ A 7 4
♣ Q 8 4 2

South
♠ K Q
♥ Q 10 9 7 4
♦ Q 8 6 2
♣ A J

West leads the ♦3 to his partner's ♦10. How do you play the hand?

With two diamond tricks in the bag, you appear to have little problem, being sure of five spades and two clubs for nine in total while you should never lose more than three hearts and the ♣K and then only if the top cards are lying badly for you. But, in this very type of situation, it is easy to take one's eye off the ball. How do you propose to play those clubs? When this hand came up, I was dummy and watched partner take his ♦Q, run the spades (overtaking on the second round) and then take the club finesse. This resulted in one down when the finesse lost and the ♦A was knocked out to leave the ♣Q stranded in an entryless dummy. At trick two, you should play the ♣A followed by the ♣J. Now nothing bad can happen.

Even if South's hearts were weaker, say ♥Q9843, so that there is a remote possibility of the defenders' taking four heart tricks, this is still the best line. The club finesse is a 50% chance. Four heart tricks will probably only be lost if East has the ♣K and West has exactly ♥AJ10x or ♥KJ10x — well under 50%.

North
♠ A J 10 9 7
♥ 6
♦ A 7 4
♣ Q 8 4 2

West
♠ 6 5 4 2
♥ K J 8
♦ K J 9 3
♣ K 6

East
♠ 8 3
♥ A 5 3 2
♦ 10 5
♣ 10 9 7 5 3

South
♠ K Q
♥ Q 10 9 7 4
♦ Q 8 6 2
♣ A J

Points to remember

1. Note the danger of blockage in these finesse positions.
2. If the finesse is to be ignored, consider the consequences of a trick lost early in the suit.

Let's move on now from no-trumps to consider the advisability of taking or avoiding the finesse in suit contracts. On a remarkable number of hands the following tip is well worth noting:

A trump finesse can be ill-advised

Dealer South
Neither vulnerable

W	N	E	S
			1♣
pass	1♦	pass	1♥
pass	2♠[1]	pass	2NT
pass	4♣	pass	6♣

[1] fourth-suit, game-forcing

North
♠ 8 6
♥ 10
♦ A K J 7 4
♣ Q J 8 6 4

South
♠ A 2
♥ A Q 9 2
♦ Q 2
♣ A 10 7 5 3

How do you play on the lead of the ♠K?

Winning the spade and finessing in trumps (the correct percentage line when considering the suit in isolation) offers a mere 50% chance of success. It is far better to play the ♣A and then, if the ♣K fails to drop, try three rounds of diamonds to get a spade discard, hoping that the hand with the long trumps can follow to diamonds at least twice. If you realised that, take most of the credit, but there is an extra chance in hearts if the trumps are 2-1: try ace and another heart, ruffing; a doubleton king could drop. Now dummy's˙losing spade can be discarded on the ♥Q.

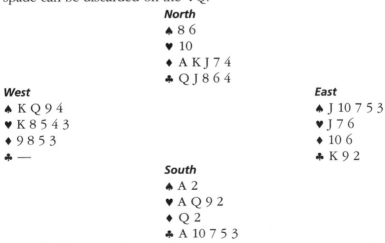

North
♠ 8 6
♥ 10
♦ A K J 7 4
♣ Q J 8 6 4

West
♠ K Q 9 4
♥ K 8 5 4 3
♦ 9 8 5 3
♣ —

East
♠ J 10 7 5 3
♥ J 7 6
♦ 10 6
♣ K 9 2

South
♠ A 2
♥ A Q 9 2
♦ Q 2
♣ A 10 7 5 3

The heart play offers a slight extra chance compared to simply hoping that diamonds are 4-2 or better. But you should refrain from playing a second heart ruff as a 6-2 heart split is slightly more likely than a 5-1 diamond split, and you are in danger of being overruffed. Note that, even if trumps are 3-0, with East having the length, as in the diagram, you still have a chance if he can follow to diamonds twice. He will ruff the third round; you overruff, return to dummy with a heart ruff and play a fourth diamond, discarding your spade loser. East can now only ruff with his winning ♣K.

Points to remember
1. Note the increased percentage gained by rejecting the trump finesse.
2. Note also the extra little chance in hearts; as indicated earlier, these little snippets add up to a lot over time.

This point is an excellent lead into the next tip:

Don't settle for half a loaf!

Finesses should be regarded with suspicion and avoided wherever possible.

Dealer East
N-S vulnerable

W	N	E	S
		pass	1♣
pass	2♦¹	pass	2NT
pass	6♣		

¹ forcing raise in clubs

North
♠ A 5 4
♥ A J 5
♦ A J
♣ A K 9 8 5

South
♠ K Q 6
♥ K 10 3
♦ Q 4
♣ Q J 10 6 2

How do you play the hand after a passive trump lead — the ♣7?

The contract seems a good one and many players would look no further than the 75% chance of one of the two finesses. The expert realises that the contract is cold, regardless of the positions of the ♦K and ♥Q. Just draw trumps and eliminate the spades before playing the ♦A and conceding a diamond trick. Whoever wins must lead hearts for you or concede a ruff and discard. If you merely take the diamond finesse, East wins and returns the suit, leaving you to guess the heart position. Similarly, if you take the heart finesse through West, East might win and return the suit, leaving you to take the diamond finesse.

North
♠ A 5 4
♥ A J 5
♦ A J
♣ A K 9 8 5

West
♠ J 9 7 2
♥ Q 9 6
♦ 10 7 6 2
♣ 7 4

East
♠ 10 8 3
♥ 8 7 4 2
♦ K 9 8 5 3
♣ 3

South
♠ K Q 6
♥ K 10 3
♦ Q 4
♣ Q J 10 6 2

Points to remember

1. Finesses should be regarded with suspicion — look for alternative lines.
2. If finesses must be taken, aim to lose to the hand which can cause you the least embarrassment. It will be instructive to alter the heart position a bit: above we had

A J 5

K 10 3

With the ten and jack present, there is no defence to the elimination and endplay but, in cases where we only have the jack, the position becomes more debatable. Consider these two lay-outs:

(a)   A J 5   (b)   A 5 4
                  or
            K 4 2   K J 2

In case (a), taking the line in the main text, you will always make the contract if East has the ♦K (he cannot profitably attack hearts) but, if West has it, (i.e. the diamond finesse was right all the time), you will go down if East has the ♥Q (unless she is singleton). It is therefore better to play three rounds of hearts instead, losing only if West has the ♥Q among three or more and East has the ♦K. Thus your chances are well over 75%.

In case (b), the line in the main text will ensure the contract if West has the ♦K (i.e. the diamond finesse is right but not necessary) because he cannot profitably attack hearts but, if East has the ♦K, we shall need the heart finesse (or a singleton ♥Q). Again, playing three rounds of hearts is a slight improvement, giving the extra chance of success if the ♥Q is doubleton over the ♥J.

Don't pay when it's free!

Now try a more advanced example on the same theme

Dealer East
N-S vulnerable

W	N	E	S
		pass	2♣
pass	2♦	pass	2NT¹
pass	3NT		

¹ 23-24 points

North
♠ 6 5
♥ 7 4
♦ 6 5 4 3
♣ Q J 9 8 2

South
♠ A Q 7
♥ K 5 3
♦ A K 7
♣ A K 6 4

How do you play the hand after West leads the ♦Q, East following with the ♦9?

There are eight tricks on top and the hand seems to be a matter of cashing the clubs and hoping for a successful spade finesse. But how about enlisting the help of the defence? If West can be forced to open up either spades or hearts, he will give you your ninth trick, free of charge. Can this be arranged?

West has, at most, five diamonds and, therefore, if you give him the lead at the right moment, you should not have to lose more than three diamond tricks and the ♥A. Try winning the first diamond and cashing three rounds of clubs. Provided West now has no more clubs, you can cash the second high diamond and exit with a third round. On the fourth and fifth diamonds, you can afford to discard a low heart and a low spade and now West must open up spades or hearts to your advantage.

North
♠ 6 5
♥ 7 4
♦ 6 5 4 3
♣ Q J 9 8 2

West
♠ K J 9
♥ A Q 9
♦ Q J 10 8 2
♣ 7 3

East
♠ 10 8 4 3 2
♥ J 10 8 6 2
♦ 9
♣ 10 5

South
♠ A Q 7
♥ K 5 3
♦ A K 7
♣ A K 6 4

Points to remember

1. Note that South must not cash all the clubs. If he does, he must discard on the fifth round and then twice more on the long diamonds, which implies blanking the ♥K or ♣A; West will exit in the appropriate suit.

Defenders are excellent guide-dogs!

Here is a further example in a suit contract where, again, the defenders can save you an awkward guess:

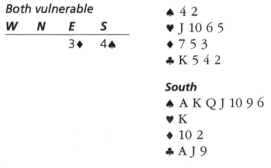

Dealer East	**North**		
Both vulnerable	♠ 4 2		

W	**N**	**E**	**S**
		3♦	4♠

North
♠ 4 2
♥ J 10 6 5
♦ 7 5 3
♣ K 5 4 2

South
♠ A K Q J 10 9 6
♥ K
♦ 10 2
♣ A J 9

West leads the ♦K, East overtaking. On the ♦Q, West discards a heart. How do you play when East persists with the ♦J?

There are nine top tricks and it seems to be a question of scoring a tenth in clubs. One approach is to take a finesse against East, a line that seems unlikely to succeed on the bidding. A second idea is to credit West with the ♣Q but hope that East has the ♣10. After drawing trumps, you run the ♣J, forcing West to cover, and then take a finesse against East's assumed ♣10. But far better is to let the defenders do the work. Ruff the third diamond high and draw trumps before exiting with the ♥K. West surely has the ♥A on the bidding and play so far. He now has the choice of giving you a free ruffing finesse in hearts or opening up the clubs.

North
♠ 4 2
♥ J 10 6 5
♦ 7 5 3
♣ K 5 4 2

West
♠ 8 7 3
♥ A Q 9 7 2
♦ K
♣ Q 10 8 7

East
♠ 5
♥ 8 4 3
♦ A Q J 9 8 6 4
♣ 6 3

South
♠ A K Q J 10 9 6
♥ K
♦ 10 2
♣ A J 9

Points to remember

1. Note how the pre-emptive bid helps to place the side-suit cards for declarer.

2. As long as West has the ♥A, the position of the ♥Q is irrelevant. In the very unlikely event of East's turning up with the ♥A, the options in clubs have not been lost.

Our next example involves taking advantage of a 'bad' distribution advertised in the auction:

Note those hazard warnings!

				North
Dealer East				♠ —
E-W vulnerable				♥ A Q 7 5 3
W	**N**	**E**	**S**	♦ K J
		pass	pass	♣ A K 7 5 4 2
2♠¹	3♠²	4♠	4NT³	
pass	6♣			**South**

¹ weak two
² strong 2-suiter
³ "pick a minor"

South

♠ 8 6
♥ 8 6 4
♦ A Q 10 7
♣ Q 10 9 3

How do you play on the lead of the ♦9?

You have eleven tricks on top and the hand seems to be a question of avoiding the loss of more than one heart trick. But there is no need to rush into the heart finesse. Draw trumps, ruffing two spades on the way, and cash the diamonds. That leaves nothing but clubs and hearts in this likely position:

North

♠ —
♥ A Q 7
♦ —
♣ 4 2

South

♠ —
♥ 8 6 4
♦ —
♣ Q 10

Now, and only now, is the time to think about hearts. The lead should be in hand and you should play a low heart, intending to play low if West fails to play the ♥9, ♥10 or ♥J. That will place the lead with East and he will have the pleasant choice of giving you a free heart finesse or a ruff and discard.

In the lay-out below, West shows out on the first heart and you play low without problem and claim.

North
♠ —
♥ A Q 7 5 3
♦ K J
♣ A K 7 5 4 2

West
♠ A Q J 10 9 4
♥ —
♦ 9 8 5 3 2
♣ 8 6

East
♠ K 7 5 3 2
♥ K J 10 9 2
♦ 6 4
♣ J

South
♠ 8 6
♥ 8 6 4
♦ A Q 10 7
♣ Q 10 9 3

But suppose West had actually played the ♥9, ♥10 or ♥J. What then? The answer lies in the count of the hand. You know that West started with six spades and the count of clubs and diamonds will have been shown in the early play. Now,

    a) if it is clear that he started with a singleton heart, you play low. Now East either overtakes, to be endplayed as before, or refuses, leaving West on play. He will then have to give you a ruff and discard — the contract must be made.

    b) if it is clear that West started with a doubleton heart, you must consider all the possibilities:

        i) if West's first heart is the ♥9, ♥10 or ♥J and his second is the ♥2, there is nothing you can do — one down;

    The same applies if West plays:

        ii) ♥9 followed by the ♥10, or the other way round,

        iii) ♥J followed by the ♥9.

    Alternatively,

        iv) if West's first heart is the ♥J and his second is the ♥10, or the other way round, then rising with the ♥A and following with a low heart ensures the contract; defenders can not organise two tricks. You will observe that, if he started with ♥J9, West must play the ♥J first or give you the contract.

    c) if it is clear that West started with three hearts, then the correct line is to play the ♥A on the first round, return to hand in trumps and only then lead low towards the ♥Q. If West has the ♥K, the contract is easy; if East has it, he will be end-played and the contract is still made.

d) If it is clear that West started with four or more hearts, then you can either play as in c) or even duck completely the first time and take a marked finesse on the second round.

So you see that it is never necessary to play a low card to the ♥Q on the first round and yet many people would do just that without giving the matter a second thought. This hand and all the possibilities will repay careful study — do not begrudge the effort.

Points to remember

1.   Note the folly of taking a first-round finesse of the ♥Q when you have better chances by playing the ♥A first.

2.   Note also the value of getting a complete count of the hand before taking a crucial decision — a priceless habit to acquire as declarer. Yes, it is an effort but there is no free lunch!

One rainy day does not make winter!

Having mastered the technique, try this next example.

Dealer East
Neither vulnerable

North
- ♠ Q J 10 5
- ♥ K Q 10
- ♦ Q 3 2
- ♣ K 7 5

W	N	E	S
		pass	1♥
2NT[1]	3NT	pass	5♥
pass	6♥		

[1] 'unusual', for the minors

South
- ♠ A K 6 2
- ♥ A 9 7 6 4 3
- ♦ A 7 4
- ♣ —

How do you play the hand on the lead of the ♦J?

If the trumps behave reasonably, you have eleven top tricks. On the auction, the ♦K should be favourably placed with West. But — no rush — how about eliminating the hand first? Win the first trick with the ♦A, cross to a high heart and ruff a club in hand. A trump to dummy is followed by a second club ruff. Then, if the trumps are 2-2, you cross to dummy in spades for a third club ruff, eliminating the suit. Cash the rest of the spades, ending in hand, and only then try a second diamond towards dummy's ♦Q.

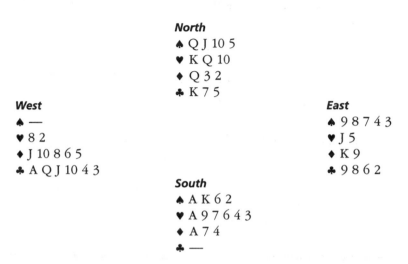

North
♠ Q J 10 5
♥ K Q 10
♦ Q 3 2
♣ K 7 5

West
♠ —
♥ 8 2
♦ J 10 8 6 5
♣ A Q J 10 4 3

East
♠ 9 8 7 4 3
♥ J 5
♦ K 9
♣ 9 8 6 2

South
♠ A K 6 2
♥ A 9 7 6 4 3
♦ A 7 4
♣ —

It loses to East's ♦K but you still survive on the above lay-out; left with nothing but black cards, East must concede a ruff and discard and the contract. Note that 6♠ is a superior contract and one that would often make an overtrick. However, here the poor spade split and favourable heart split result in 6♥ being made while 6♠ is difficult.

Points to remember
1)   Note the delay in playing the critical suit.
2)   It is virtually never right to play the ♦Q at trick one. If the ♦K is favourably placed, the ♦Q's trick will not run away. Meanwhile, even if the endplay does not work, there is always the chance that East's ♦K could be singleton.
3)   Despite West's known length in the minors, there is no law that says he has to hold the ♦K. Be careful of such assumptions when there are alternative lines of play.

In this next hand, the timing of drawing trumps is crucial.

Catch the loner at the right moment!

Dealer East
E-W vulnerable

W	N	E	S
		1♦	2♥
pass	3♥	pass	4♥

North
♠ A 5
♥ 10 9 8
♦ 7 4
♣ K 8 7 5 4 2

South
♠ K J 8
♥ Q J 7 6 5 3 2
♦ A
♣ J 10

How do you play on the lead of the ♦6 to East's ♦9?

The clubs are probably badly placed and you may already have been lucky to have avoided a club lead.   Now you must capitalise on your good fortune.   Look at that trump position.   East could well have a singleton trump honour.   In that case, the first round of trumps would leave him on lead and your job is to make it as embarrassing as possible.

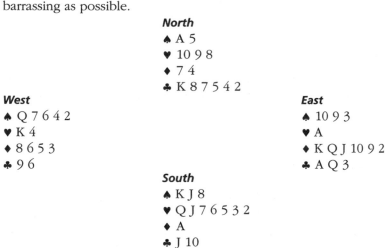

North
♠ A 5
♥ 10 9 8
♦ 7 4
♣ K 8 7 5 4 2

West
♠ Q 7 6 4 2
♥ K 4
♦ 8 6 5 3
♣ 9 6

East
♠ 10 9 3
♥ A
♦ K Q J 10 9 2
♣ A Q 3

South
♠ K J 8
♥ Q J 7 6 5 3 2
♦ A
♣ J 10

On winning the diamond, cross to the ♠A and ruff dummy's last diamond to eliminate the suit. Now the ♠K is followed by a spade ruff. Only now do you lead a trump and, in the above lay-out, East is endplayed, forced to open up the clubs to your advantage or concede a ruff and discard.

Points to remember

1.   The elimination play costs nothing. In the unlikely event of defenders' interfering, it will be with trump tricks which are theirs anyway.
2.   If all else fails, the chance of the ♣Q being with West has not been lost.

Cover no more than necessary!

Try this next example where, again, the auction makes it plain that an ace is badly placed for you:

Dealer East
Neither vulnerable

W	N	E	S
		pass	1♦
1♥	1♠	2♥	2♠
3♥	4♦	pass	5♦

North
♠ A Q J 7
♥ J 5 4
♦ A 10 4
♣ 9 6 5

South
♠ K 10 6
♥ —
♦ K Q 8 7 6 5
♣ K 10 8 4

How do you play on the lead of the ♥K?

The opening lead has marked the position of the ♥A in the East hand, and therefore the ♣A is almost certainly with West and you are in danger of losing three club tricks.   Leading a club towards the king is, therefore, out of the question.   A better alternative would be to finesse clubs twice (leading first the ♣9, and then, if that lost, playing up to the ♣10), hoping to find East with the queen or jack. But better still is to arrange for an endplay.   South's possession of the ♣10 makes the contract a certainty if the trumps break 2-2 and the necessary groundwork is prepared.   Ruff the heart lead and draw trumps, ending in dummy.   Ruff a second heart, cross to dummy in spades and ruff dummy's last heart.   Finish the spades and lead a club from dummy, intending just to cover whatever East puts on. West must win and then either give you a ruff and discard or continue clubs to give you a free finesse.

	North	
	♠ A Q J 7	
	♥ J 5 4	
	♦ A 10 4	
	♣ 9 6 5	

West		**East**
♠ 8 3		♠ 9 5 4 2
♥ K Q 10 8 6 2		♥ A 9 7 3
♦ 9 3		♦ J 2
♣ A Q J		♣ 7 3 2

	South	
	♠ K 10 6	
	♥ —	
	♦ K Q 8 7 6 5	
	♣ K 10 8 4	

The question now arises as to how to play if the trumps are 3-1 — what then? The best line in this case is probably to draw all the trumps and take two finesses in clubs; East may well have at least one of the ♣Q and ♣J.

Points to remember

1. Note how the line of play varies with the trump break.
2. A point for the defenders, admittedly irrelevant on this hand but often applicable: East should at least consider overtaking his partner's lead. Assuming South can follow the suit once, this would be his only chance for an entry to play clubs at an early stage; an endplay might thus be avoided.

4

Reading the Opponents

In most sports and games and in many professions, notably the legal and military, few considerations are more important than knowledge of the enemy. At the bridge table, the declarer faces two enemies and must consider which is the more dangerous and when!

Length demands early attack!

At no-trumps, if the lead has to be lost more than once, the entry of the defender with the long suit should be eliminated first. This is another illustration of the importance of playing a hand through mentally before touching a card:

Dealer West				**North**
Neither vulnerable				♠ 7 6
W	**N**	**E**	**S**	♥ A Q J
pass	1♣	3♠	3NT	♦ Q J 10 7
				♣ K 5 4 3

South
♠ A Q
♥ 10 9 3 2
♦ K 8 6 2
♣ A 8 6

How do you play on the lead of the ♠10, East playing the ♠J?

Beginners are taught that *inevitable* losers should be lost before *possible* losers. The ♦A is inevitable while the ♥K may be avoided if the finesse is right. It might be argued, therefore, that declarer should start on diamonds. But playing the hand through mentally will guide you to the right track. If the heart finesse is right, there is no problem, so place the ♥K with East. Now, if you start on diamonds, West may win and play a second spade. You do not have enough tricks without the hearts and a losing finesse now would result in a string of spades being cashed against you.

So try the heart finesse first. If it holds, switch to diamonds to ensure nine tricks. If it loses, East will return a spade which you win but now playing on diamonds will put West on play (East can hardly have both red honours, having pre-empted and, if he has, you had no chance anyway).

Assuming that East has seven spades for his pre-empt, West will now have no spade left to lead when he is in with the ♦A, and you will make nine tricks in comfort.

                          North
                          ♠ 7 6
                          ♥ A Q J
                          ♦ Q J 10 7
                          ♣ K 5 4 3
West   **East**
♠ 10 3   ♠ K J 9 8 5 4 2
♥ 8 7 5 4   ♥ K 6
♦ A 9 4   ♦ 5 3
♣ Q 10 9 2   ♣ J 7
                          South
                          ♠ A Q
                          ♥ 10 9 3 2
                          ♦ K 8 6 2
                          ♣ A 8 6

Points to remember

1. Note the importance of mentally placing the cards, *in a manner consistent with the bidding and early play*, before choosing your line of play.
2. Following 1), note the sequence of play to lose tricks to opponents in the correct order.

Watch the other bidders in the auction room!

For both declarer and, even more important, defenders, attention to the bidding can hardly be overemphasised. Use the information available from the following auction to help pin-point the opponents' cards.

Dealer South
N-S vulnerable

W	N	E	S
			1♠
pass	2♠	pass	3♦¹
pass	4♠		

¹ help-suit game try

North

♠ Q J 4 3
♥ Q 8 3
♦ Q 7 6 4
♣ Q 2

South

♠ A K 10 9 7
♥ 10
♦ K 8 5 2
♣ A 7 3

North's 4♠ was, in my opinion, ill-advised. Despite being maximum for his raise and holding the ♦Q, he should have declined the invitation. There are two reasons for this: firstly, North's values are 'soft' (queens and jacks rather than aces and kings), and secondly, the ♥Q and ♣Q are likely to be of little value facing probable shortness.

So you are in a bad contract but now you have to try to make it after West cashes the ♥A and switches to the ♣J. You try the ♣Q from dummy, but East produces the ♣K. Both defenders follow to two rounds of trumps. How do you place the cards?

The opening lead marks West with the ♥K. So he has already shown eight points in the ♥A, ♥K and ♣J. If he has the ♦A as well, that would give him twelve and about enough for a take-out double of your opening 1♠ bid; he may well have the right shape for it. *But West took no action over your opening bid.* It is, therefore, probable that East has the ♦A and, because of the tenuous position in that suit, you must assume that he has exactly a doubleton. You thus should play a low diamond towards the ♦K in hand and duck completely on the way back to try to restrict your losses to one heart, one diamond, and the inevitable club.

North
♠ Q J 4 3
♥ Q 8 3
♦ Q 7 6 4
♣ Q 2

West
♠ 8 5
♥ A K J 5
♦ J 9 3
♣ J 10 8 6

East
♠ 6 2
♥ 9 7 6 4 2
♦ A 10
♣ K 9 5 4

South
♠ A K 10 9 7
♥ 10
♦ K 8 5 2
♣ A 7 3

Points to remember

1) Try to place the cards from the opponents' bidding *and that includes their passes*.

2) The contract is poor, dependent on a 3-2 diamond split with East having the doubleton ♦A (about 13.5%). In a poor contract, place the cards where you must to give you a chance of success and play accordingly, but note that this must be consistent with the bidding and early play.

The dog that didn't bark!

Dealer East
E-W vulnerable

W	N	E	S
		pass	1♥
pass	2♣	pass	2♥
pass	3♥	pass	4♥

North
♠ J 5
♥ K 10 2
♦ 5 4 3
♣ A Q J 8 7

South
♠ Q 2
♥ A J 6 5 4 3
♦ A 8 6
♣ K 5

Sherlock Holmes solved one of his most famous cases by noticing the curious fact that a dog did not bark while the crime was being committed. As we have just seen, silence can be most enlightening at the bridge table too. This hand is another example.

West leads the ♠10 and East cashes the ♠K and ♠A before switching to the ♦Q, West encouraging with the ♦7 as you win with the ♦A. How do you play now?

East has already shown up with nine points and probably the ♦J to make ten. With the ♥Q as well, he would be likely to have opened the bidding, so West is a hot favourite to hold that card.

North
♠ J 5
♥ K 10 2
♦ 5 4 3
♣ A Q J 8 7

West
♠ 10 9 8 7 3
♥ Q 8 7
♦ K 7 2
♣ 10 3

East
♠ A K 6 4
♥ 9
♦ Q J 10 9
♣ 9 6 4 2

South
♠ Q 2
♥ A J 6 5 4 3
♦ A 8 6
♣ K 5

Points to remember

1. Get into the habit of counting defenders' points as they play their high cards; as before, their bidding, or the lack of it, may be a mine of information — tap it!

2. As a defender, do not be in a rush to cash winners if doing so will give declarer helpful informaition. Of course, here, if East fails to cash his spades, South can discard a loser on the third round of clubs. But it would have been better for East to lead a deceptive ♦J or ♦10 at trick three, 'placing' the high honours in the West hand. Now there is room for the ♥Q to be with East, and South is quite likely to be defeated. His best line is to play two top hearts and follow with clubs, hoping that, if the ♥Q has failed to fall, she is accompanied by at least three clubs, giving declarer time to get rid of his diamond losers. On this layout however, he will not be lucky.

The wrong way is the right way!

Information from the bidding may help when there is a choice of plays in a single suit. In this next example, we illustrate a position calling for an unusual type of finesse.

Dealer North
Neither vulnerable

W	N	E	S
	1♥	1NT[1]	dbl
2♣	pass	pass	3NT

[1] 15-17 points

North
♠ A J 9
♥ A J 9 8 7
♦ Q 6 3
♣ 6 2

South
♠ K Q 8 6
♥ K 3
♦ 10 9 8 7 2
♣ A 8

West leads the ♣J to his partner's ♣Q and you allow it to hold. East cashes the ♦K and continues with the ♣K which you have to win. How do you play from here?

There are twenty-four points on view and West has already shown up with the ♣J, leaving the remainder for his partner. The normal heart finesse is obviously a certain way to defeat. But, while it is certain that East has the ♥Q, there is a chance that West has the ♥10, in which case crossing to dummy in spades and playing the ♥J from there secures five tricks in the suit if it breaks 3-3. East will be forced to cover, and you will win the king. You are now left with the A 9 in dummy, and by leading towards it, you can take a straightforward finesse against West's ♥10.

This type of play is more often used by defenders, typically in positions where East sits with A J 9 or K J 9 over dummy's 10 x x and has reason to place South with the queen and partner with the outstanding high honour. The lead of the jack through declarer's queen leaves West on lead, and East holding A9 or K9 over dummy's ten will take the next two tricks in the suit. The technical name for this stratagem is a 'surround play'.

North
♠ A J 9
♥ A J 9 8 7
♦ Q 6 3
♣ 6 2

West
♠ 5 4 3
♥ 10 5 2
♦ 5
♣ J 10 9 7 4 3

East
♠ 10 7 2
♥ Q 6 4
♦ A K J 4
♣ K Q 5

South
♠ K Q 8 6
♥ K 3
♦ 10 9 8 7 2
♣ A 8

Points to remember

1. East's 1NT bid places him with a heart stopper and therefore the ♥Q. Ruling out psychic bidding, the normal finesse offers a 0% chance rather than the usual 50%.

2. Be on the look-out for these two-way finesse positions lower down the order. Here we had

```
                    A J 9 8 7
        10 5 2                        Q 6 4
                    K 3
```

A similar approach applies with

```
                    Q 7 5 2
        A J 4                         9 6 3
                    K 10 8
```

In the absence of information suggesting the contrary, the normal approach would be low to the queen and finesse the ten against the jack on the way back. But, if you have good reason to place the jack with West, lead the ten from hand, forcing him to cover. Subsequently, take a finesse against East's presumed nine. Note that the position of the ace is irrelevant!

Speed is the mother of theft!

Knowledge of opponents' holdings and intentions is especially important in the context of timing of winning tricks. When the race is on, look for opportunities to steal; defenders must be particularly alert.

Dealer North
E-W vulnerable

W	N	E	S
	pass	1♣[1]	dbl
pass	1♥	pass	2NT
pass	3NT		

[1] natural; E-W play a 15-17
  1NT opening

North

♠ Q 5 2
♥ 10 9 6 3
♦ K 8 7
♣ 9 3 2

South

♠ K J 7 3
♥ Q J 5
♦ A Q J
♣ A K Q

West leads the ♣6. How do you play the hand?

There are plenty of tricks but you will have to lose the lead several times to establish them. Meanwhile, the defenders (here specifically East) are threatening to take two club tricks, assuming East started with at least a five-card suit, plus the two top hearts and ♠A. If the spades are 3-3, there is no problem as you can take nine tricks without touching hearts. But if not, you could be in trouble.

It is clear that East must have all the outstanding honour cards so the correct line, after winning the club lead in hand perforce, is to overtake the ♦J in dummy before leading a low spade from there. Now East is caught between the devil and the deep blue sea — the position is known as 'Morton's Fork'. If East rises with the ♠A, you will have three spade tricks, irrespective of the break, to go with three clubs and three diamonds and you needn't touch the hearts. If he ducks, you will win the spade in hand and, having stolen a trick without losing the lead, you will switch to hearts to take two heart tricks, the one spade, three clubs and three diamonds.

On this line of play, East can try winning the first heart and persisting with clubs, ducking the second heart to isolate dummy and prevent your enjoying a second heart trick. But if he does so, you have now stolen a heart trick and can revert to spades to ensure two spade tricks, one heart, and three in each minor!

North
♠ Q 5 2
♥ 10 9 6 3
♦ K 8 7
♣ 9 3 2

West
♠ 10 8 6 4
♥ 8 7 4
♦ 10 5 3 2
♣ 6 4

East
♠ A 9
♥ A K 2
♦ 9 6 4
♣ J 10 8 7 5

South
♠ K J 7 3
♥ Q J 5
♦ A Q J
♣ A K Q

Points to remember

1. Note the importance of counting the tricks available to *both declarer and defenders* and the number of times the lead will change hands in race situations — this especially applies at no-trumps.

2. The play in spades is a typical example of the advantage of leading from weakness through strength to strength, a stratagem you should use as often as possible.

Communications

Issues

5

Handling Entries

We shall now concentrate on contracts, usually at no-trumps, where there is a race between declarer and the defenders to see who can establish their tricks first. Often declarer must put his opponents in a position where it is too expensive to keep up the chase. We shall start with a position where one hand is markedly stronger than the other and there are consequent communication problems.

Don't block the artery — survival may depend on it!

Entries should be treasured, especially in situations where they are sparse in one hand. In this example, it appears to cost nothing to take a finesse.

Dealer North
N-S vulnerable

W	N	E	S
	2♣	pass	2♦
pass	2♠	pass	2NT
pass	4NT	pass	6NT

North
♠ A K Q 3
♥ A J 6
♦ A K 6 4
♣ A K

South
♠ 5 2
♥ Q 10 7
♦ 8 7 3
♣ Q J 10 7 6

Following a poor bidding sequence, you play 6NT from the South hand. How do you play if West leads the ♥5 and would it make any difference if North were declarer and East led the ♥5?

Either way, the club suit has to be brought in and, with the blockage in the big hand, the only hope of an entry lies in hearts. For that reason, the ♥A must be played to remove it from the stage as soon as possible, while the ♥ Q 10 are kept intact. If dummy plays low at trick one, a good player sitting East may withhold his ♥K, leaving the South hand dead; the contract probably goes two off.

In the situation where North is declarer, and East leads a heart, dummy (South) must again play low, keeping the two honours intact. West also plays low and North must win the ♥A. Cash the two club honours and overtake the ♥J with ♥Q or lead low to the ♥10 to gain entry to the South hand.

Points to remember
1. Do not get too excited on huge hands, where the combined strength is massed on one side; often there are insuperable entry problems. 2NT openers which get passed out very often fail to make their contract.
2. Look for every opportunity to create an entry to the weak hand. Spectacular unblocks are often needed.

A crime unpunished is still a crime!

We shall now turn to positions where entries should be handled carefully, because ruffs are needed early in the play.

Dealer West   **North**
N-S vulnerable   ♠ 8 4

W	N	E	S
2♠¹	dbl	pass	6♥
pass	7♥		

¹ 6 spades, 4-9 points

North
♠ 8 4
♥ K Q 4
♦ A K Q 9
♣ K 6 5 2

South
♠ A K 9
♥ A 9 8 6 3
♦ 6 5
♣ A 7 3

How do you play on the lead of the ♣J?

If trumps are 4-1, you are almost certainly doomed, Even if West has a singleton ♥10 or ♥J, you will not be able to take a spade ruff in dummy and pick up East's trumps, so you will need a miracle in diamonds to bring home the slam.   Assuming a 3-2 trump split, then, you have twelve tricks on top and all that is needed is one spade ruff. In order to manage this safely, you must assume that East has exactly two trumps (since he is known to have only two spades from the auction), and you will need to draw two rounds of trumps before the ruff. You must be careful with entries, treasuring the club entry to your hand by winning the first trick in dummy.   Then the ♥K and ♥Q are followed by two top spades and the ruff. Returning to hand with the ♣A, you can draw the last trump and claim.

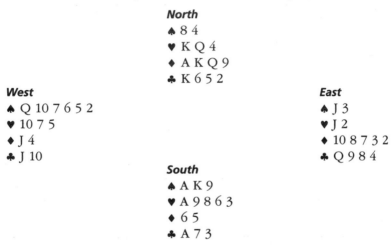

North
♠ 8 4
♥ K Q 4
♦ A K Q 9
♣ K 6 5 2

West
♠ Q 10 7 6 5 2
♥ 10 7 5
♦ J 4
♣ J 10

East
♠ J 3
♥ J 2
♦ 10 8 7 3 2
♣ Q 9 8 4

South
♠ A K 9
♥ A 9 8 6 3
♦ 6 5
♣ A 7 3

Observe what happened when a 'world-class' player was declarer on a similar hand. He won the first club in hand and drew two rounds of trumps with the ♥K and ♥Q. He then realised, to his horror, that it was now no longer possible to take the spade ruff and return to hand safely to draw last trump. With any justice, the contract would have gone one down but the actual diamond position was:

                        A K Q 9
        J 10   8 7 4 3 2
                        6 5

The suit came in for four tricks and declarer's trick one mistake went unpunished.

Points to remember

1. Note the necessary assumption about the trump situation. If East has three trumps, the hand cannot be made unless there is a miracle in diamonds.

2. Note the necessity of keeping the club entry to hand. Hasty play to the first trick could cost the contract.

3. A case could be made for playing one top diamond at trick two, in case the miracle exists. If West drops the ♦10 or ♦J, declarer could decide to play for the miracle rather than for East to have exactly two trumps. However, West could have a singleton diamond, and even if he has two or three, it costs him nothing to drop an honour on the first round. Apart from the risk of a ruff, South cannot afford a second test round of diamonds since he will need the ♦K as a dummy entry after taking the spade ruff and drawing trumps.

It costs nothing to give nothing!

On other occasions, a trick may even have to be 'sacrificed', as in this example.

Dealer South
N-S vulnerable

W	N	E	S
			2♣
pass	2♦	pass	2♥
pass	3♥	pass	3♠
pass	4♦	pass	4NT
pass	5♦	pass	6♥

North
♠ 8 6
♥ 7 6 2
♦ A K 7 5
♣ J 10 4 3

South
♠ A Q 9
♥ K Q 10 9 5 3
♦ Q 6
♣ A K

How do play on the lead of the ♦J?

With a certain trump loser, you will have to assume that the spade finesse is right but, even then, there is the further problem of a possible second trump loser. If both the ace and jack of trumps are offside among three, there is no chance but, if they are both with East, you will need to play trumps through him twice. Entries to dummy are thus priceless as three finesses may be needed.

Strangely enough, the contract would be easier without that ♦Q as there would be no temptation to win trick one in hand. You must win in dummy and play a trump towards the ♥K. If it holds, overtake in diamonds, take the spade finesse, cash the ♦A and take a spade ruff before playing another trump through East. Note that, with the ruff available, the extra diamond trick given up was of no value.

North
♠ 8 6
♥ 7 6 2
♦ A K 7 5
♣ J 10 4 3

West
♠ 7 5 4 3
♥ 8
♦ J 10 9 4
♣ Q 7 6 5

East
♠ K J 10 2
♥ A J 4
♦ 8 3 2
♣ 9 8 2

South
♠ A Q 9
♥ K Q 10 9 5 3
♦ Q 6
♣ A K

Points to remember

1. The diamond position apparently offers a discard, but make sure it is needed before you insist on taking it. Here the alternative spade ruff enables declarer to win a trick in dummy, where the entry is crucial.
2. Note the trump position; if the first round loses, you will have to take a decision on the second, but, where possible, the first round should be played from dummy to protect against a singleton ace with East.

Drawing trumps must know its time and place!

I mentioned earlier that the technique of finessing was taught to beginners at an early stage but that later they were taught how to avoid finesses. A similar progression applies to drawing trumps, although the word 'avoid' will normally be replaced by 'delay'. The scarcity of entries to dummy may be an important consideration when deciding how many rounds of trumps to draw; it is easy to go wrong on this next example:

Dealer North
Neither vulnerable

W	N	E	S
	1♠	2♣	2♦
5♣	pass	pass	5♦

North
♠ A Q 7 5 2
♥ K 5 3
♦ K 3 2
♣ 9 4

South
♠ 9 4
♥ A J 7
♦ A Q 10 9 7 5 4
♣ 2

West leads the ♣6 and East's ♣K wins. You ruff the ♣A, West playing the ♣5, and cash the ♦A, on which West discards the ♣7. How do you continue?

You have seven trump tricks and three side-suit winners so it appears that a successful finesse in either major will see you home. But the spade suit offers an extra chance. A 4-2 or better break will enable you to set up a long card, provided you keep enough entries. Even one more round of trumps, keeping the ♦K in dummy, is premature. East will win and play a third round of trumps; you now lack the entries to cash the long spade. You are left at the mercy of the heart finesse and justice will have been done when it fails.

North
♠ A Q 7 5 2
♥ K 5 3
♦ K 3 2
♣ 9 4

West
♠ 8 6
♥ Q 10 9 8 6 2
♦ —
♣ Q 8 7 6 5

East
♠ K J 10 3
♥ 4
♦ J 8 6
♣ A K J 10 3

South
♠ 9 4
♥ A J 7
♦ A Q 10 9 7 5 4
♣ 2

Now, instead, try taking the spade finesse before a second round of trumps: East cannot hurt you. A trump or a heart will be won in hand and you will play the ♠A, ruff a spade, finish trumps in dummy and ruff a fourth spade. Now you return to the ♥K to enjoy the fifth spade, on which you discard your potentially losing heart.

Points to remember

1. Note particularly the trump entry position and that the ♦K must not only be left in dummy but must be protected from premature attack by the company of a low trump.

2. In the unlikely event of the spades being 5-1, the heart finesse chance has not been lost. The only layout in which this line loses as against two simple finesses is one where East has a singleton ♣K and the ♥Q — much less likely than the actual lie.

Having seen the idea, try to anticipate the problem on this next hand.

The side suit takes precedence!

Dealer South
E-W vulnerable

W	N	E	S
			1♠
pass	1NT	pass	2♣
pass	5♣		

North
♠ K 7
♥ 10 5 3
♦ A 3
♣ Q 7 6 4 3 2

South
♠ A 8 5 4 2
♥ 7 2
♦ Q 4
♣ A K 10 9

West leads the ♣8, East playing the ♣5. Plan the play.

With three potential red-suit losers, you will need to set up a long spade for a diamond discard. There is little problem if spades are 3-3 and no chance if they are 5-1 or worse. The critical case arises in the most likely case of a 4-2 break. Try drawing a second round of trumps and playing on spades. After the third round, ruffed in dummy, you return to hand in trumps and ruff a fourth round. You return to hand in trumps again but are now out of trumps in both hands and cannot benefit from the diamond discard.

Thus you must work on spades immediately. Win the first trump in hand, and play three rounds of spades, ruffing high to prevent an overruff by East. Now play a second trump and ruff a fourth spade. A third trump gets you back to hand to enjoy the established spade.

North
♠ K 7
♥ 10 5 3
♦ A 3
♣ Q 7 6 4 3 2

West
♠ Q 10 9 6
♥ K J 6
♦ K 10 8 7 6
♣ 8

East
♠ J 3
♥ A Q 9 8 4
♦ J 9 5 2
♣ J 5

South
♠ A 8 5 4 2
♥ 7 2
♦ Q 4
♣ A K 10 9

Points to remember

1. Note the win of the first trump *in hand* to prevent the overruff on the third round of spades. Be on the lookout for these little precautions.

Once is enough!

Dealer North
E-W vulnerable

W	N	E	S
	1♦	pass	1♥
pass	3♥	pass	3NT
pass	4♥		

North
♠ 5 3
♥ A K Q 10
♦ A Q 7 5 3
♣ 7 6

South
♠ K Q 8
♥ 9 8 6 2
♦ 9 4
♣ K 9 5 3

Some will argue over South's 'correct' response to 1♦ on this hand. There are still those who insist that the hearts are 'not good enough to bid' and prefer 1NT. In my view, this is ill-advised for a number of reasons:

- a) as here, North may not be strong enough to reverse over a 1NT response and now a heart contract may be missed.
- b) if the final contract is 3NT, you may want it played from the other side if partner has something like ♣Qx or ♥Kx or ♥AQ.
- c) if you do eventually play 3NT from your side, you may well avoid a lethal heart lead.

West leads the ♣Q to his partner's ♣A and the East returns the ♠2. You play the ♠K but West wins with the ♠A and returns the ♠10 which you win. You try a low diamond to the ♦Q but East wins and you have to ruff the ♠J in dummy. How do you continue?

You need the rest, but ruffing any more black cards in dummy is out as that would probably allow the defenders a trick with the ♥J. The diamonds have to be ruffed high and the trump honours in dummy are the only entries. You need to assume that trumps break 3-2 and that diamonds are no worse than 4-2, with the ♥J in the hand with the long diamonds. With two entries needed in dummy to establish and cash the long diamond, you can only afford one round of trumps at this stage. Then the ♦A is followed by a diamond ruff, a trump honour and another diamond, if necessary.   Finally, return to the last trump honour in dummy to cash the long diamond to complete six trump tricks, two diamonds and two black honours.

North
♠ 5 3
♥ A K Q 10
♦ A Q 7 5 3
♣ 7 6

West
♠ A 10 9 6 4
♥ 5 3
♦ 10 6
♣ Q J 10 4

East
♠ J 7 2
♥ J 7 4
♦ K J 8 2
♣ A 8 2

South
♠ K Q 8
♥ 9 8 6 2
♦ 9 4
♣ K 9 5 3

Points to remember

1. The line of play was largely dictated by the presence of very good trumps in one hand opposite low cards in the other. Had the big trumps all been with South, you might have had to consider ruffing two club losers in dummy.

2. Note that the defenders forced dummy with spades, trying to restrict the number of entries to the diamonds.

Don't block the highway!

It is very easy to take tricks for granted, particularly when, in a specific suit, there are few high cards in enemy hands. A special effort should be made to ensure that tricks which are rightfully yours can be cashed. When you have an isolated long suit, beware of blockages. It is very easy to start bashing out winners, only to find that, too late, you have run into a brick wall. As before, insist on playing the hand out mentally before touching a single card. The following situation illustrates the minefield in this area.

Dealer East
E-W vulnerable

W	N	E	S
		pass	1NT
2♣	3NT		

North
♠ 9 4 3
♥ 9 2
♦ A K 5 4 2
♣ A 4 2

South
♠ K J 10 7
♥ A K Q
♦ Q 9 7 6
♣ 8 3

West leads the ♣K, East playing the ♣J. Plan the play.

It seems that, barring an unlikely 4-0 diamond break, there are five diamond tricks, one club and three hearts. So you win the club lead and . . . . go one down! Now look at the diamonds more closely; there is no problem if they split 2-2 but, if they are 3-1, what happens on the fourth round? South has to win and there is no entry to the fifth winner. South's blocking card needs to be discarded early and this can only be done on the ♣A! Duck the first club, refuse the second round and win the third, discarding a diamond to clear the road to nine tricks.

North
♠ 9 4 3
♥ 9 2
♦ A K 5 4 2
♣ A 4 2

West
♠ A Q 2
♥ J 10 3
♦ 3
♣ K Q 10 9 7 5

East
♠ 8 6 5
♥ 8 7 6 5 4
♦ J 10 8
♣ J 6

South
♠ K J 10 7
♥ A K Q
♦ Q 9 7 6
♣ 8 3

Points to remember

1. Always look for trouble of this kind when you have an isolated long suit in one hand.
2. Consider what happens if West refuses to co-operate, switching to hearts at trick two. Incredibly, you must play another club yourself, ducking. Win the heart return, cross to the diamonds and take your discard on the ♣A.

CHAPTER

6

Disrupting the Defence

Here we shall consider a number of stratagems that declarer can use to frustrate enemy intentions and learn to distinguish between appropriate and inappropriate occasions for their use.

Enjoy the pond with discretion!

Bridge players are taught at an early stage that it is not necessarily correct to win a trick at the first opportunity. However, ducking has its time and place! The purpose of ducking is to cut defenders' communications. Do not duck without good reason.

Dealer North
N-S vulnerable

W	N	E	S
	1♦	pass	2♦
2♠	dbl	pass	3NT

North
♠ K Q 10 5
♥ A Q 4
♦ A K 7 2
♣ 6 3

South
♠ 3
♥ 9 7 3
♦ Q J 10 9 4
♣ A 9 8 5

How would you play on the lead of the ♣K, East playing the ♣7?

Most players would duck without giving the matter a second thought but there has to be a reason. What is the purpose of ducking? First, ask yourself what the club situation is. Even if West has five and East two, West will always have the ♠A as entry and you achieve nothing by ducking in an attempt to exhaust East. Count your tricks. You have five diamonds, the ♥A and ♣A and can easily set up one trick in spades. Thus, if the heart finesse is right, there is no problem. If it is wrong, then ducking trick one could be fatal.

North
♠ K Q 10 5
♥ A Q 4
♦ A K 7 2
♣ 6 3

West
♠ A J 9 7 6 2
♥ 8 6 2
♦ —
♣ K Q 10 4

East
♠ 8 4
♥ K J 10 5
♦ 8 6 5 3
♣ J 7 2

South
♠ 3
♥ 9 7 3
♦ Q J 10 9 4
♣ A 9 8 5

West will switch to hearts at trick two and your finesse will lose. Then East will return to clubs to complete five tricks for the defenders before you have set up any spade tricks. To combat this, you should win trick one and play a spade towards the ten. If it holds, as it almost certainly will, play a spade honour next to ensure two spade tricks to join your seven top winners.

Points to remember
1. Ducking in no-trumps is common practice and very often right but do not do so without good reason; consider the possibility of a dangerous switch.
2. Never forget to count your own and the potential enemy tricks before deciding whether to win or duck.

Charity begins at home!

The principle of losing the first trick in a suit applies in a suit contract when you are threatened with too many losers and need to
assume that one defender can be run out of entries:

Dealer East				North
E-W vulnerable				♠ A 5 3 2
W	**N**	**E**	**S**	♥ J 10 5 4
		pass	1♥	♦ 5 3
pass	3♥	pass	4♥	♣ A 4 3

South
♠ Q
♥ A K Q 3 2
♦ Q J 10 6
♣ 8 7 5

How do play on the lead of the ♣K?

You have four obvious losers and there seems no way to discard any
of them in time. The only hope is to find East with both the two top
diamond honours so that West cannot get in to cash his clubs. How
about the club distribution? If they are 4-3, you have no chance
but, if they are 5-2, refusing the first round will exhaust East and
cut the defenders' communications. Win the second round, draw
trumps and play on diamonds to ensure a club discard.

        North
        ♠ A 5 3 2
        ♥ J 10 5 4
        ♦ 5 3
        ♣ A 4 3

West		*East*
♠ J 10 7 4		♠ K 9 8 6
♥ 9		♥ 8 7 6
♦ 7 4 2		♦ A K 9 8
♣ K Q 10 9 2		♣ J 6

        South
        ♠ Q
        ♥ A K Q 3 2
        ♦ Q J 10 6
        ♣ 8 7 5

Of course, if the clubs are 6-1, you have to win the first rather than the second round but, in the absence of any bidding to suggest the contrary, you should assume the 5-2 break which is much more likely.

Points to remember

1. When in a poor contract, place the high cards and distribution to give yourself the best chance.
2. Note that, if the contract were 5♥, you would be correct to win the first round of clubs. Now you cannot afford even one club loser and must assume the unlikely 6-1 split.

Lose the battle, win the war!

The idea of losing an early round in a suit might be put just this way. This applies to both declarer and defenders — where a long suit is being set up, it is usually right to lose an early round to maintain your communications or, where appropriate, ruin those of the enemy! This primarily applies to no-trump contracts but, as we just saw, suit contracts are by no means exempt. Here's another no-trump example.

Dealer North	**North**
Neither vulnerable	♠ A K 2

W	**N**	**E**	**S**
	1♣	1♥	1NT
pass	3NT		

North
♠ A K 2
♥ Q J 2
♦ A K J
♣ J 10 9 2

South
♠ Q 5 4
♥ A 7 6
♦ 10 9 4
♣ K 8 7 5

West leads the ♥8. How do you play the hand?

You have three top spades, two hearts, and at most three diamonds so you will need at least one and probably two club tricks, the diamond finesse being a likely failure.   East almost certainly has the ♣A and, if he has the ♣Q as well, there is no problem.   The critical case arises when West has the ♣Q.   Suppose you put on a heart honour from dummy at trick one, and East ducks (he gains nothing by covering).   Now a club finesse, losing to West's ♣Q, is followed by another heart and your second stopper will be knocked out.   On regaining the lead with the ♣A, East will cash two more hearts to complete five tricks for the defenders.

But now try the effect of *insisting on losing* the first heart.   Play low from both hands.   Win the second round and then take the club finesse, losing to West.   He is now out of hearts (if he isn't, they have split 4-3 and you were never in danger anyway) and must switch to another suit to put you a tempo ahead.

North
♠ A K 2
♥ Q J 2
♦ A K J
♣ J 10 9 2

West
♠ 10 8 7 6 3
♥ 8 5
♦ 8 5 3 2
♣ Q 6

East
♠ J 9
♥ K 10 9 4 3
♦ Q 7 6
♣ A 4 3

South
♠ Q 5 4
♥ A 7 6
♦ 10 9 4
♣ K 8 7 5

Points to remember — and there are several

1. Note the importance to both declarer and defender of losing the first round of hearts.

2. A point often missed, even by the experts — look at that defenders' club situation carefully: it was

Q 6   opposite   A 4 3

In this case, declarer could not avoid losing the first of his two losers to the ♣Q. But suppose it had been

Q 6 3   opposite   A 4

Now, even if declarer misplays the hearts, he can save himself by rising with the ♣K on the first round. The first loss will be to East's ♣A and declarer is now out of danger.

3. After South plays correctly at trick one, West might realise that the game is up as far as hearts are concerned and might switch to diamonds, going for two diamonds, a heart and two clubs. How does South play now? Try it both ways: if he finesses diamonds, East wins and returns the suit. It is now in the interest of the defenders that East wins the first club trick to return a third diamond while West's ♣Q is kept intact as an entry for the thirteenth winning diamond. He will rise with ♣A on the first round and the defence will prevail in the case where West has the ♣Q trebleton or longer. If South takes the ♦A at trick two, he is better placed. Now, if East wins the first club, he cannot profitably continue diamonds and, if West wins the first club and continues diamonds, he can never come to his long diamond, regardless of how South plays.

Dangerous criminals should be locked away ... early!

We shall now consider further ways of ruining enemy communications. As we have already emphasised, tricks must be lost to the right people at the right time:

Dealer East *Neither vulnerable*				**North**
W	**N**	**E**	**S**	♠ K 8 4 2
		1♠	3♥[1]	♥ 10
dbl[2]				♦ Q 8 3
[1] intermediate				♣ A 7 6 3 2
[2] penalties				

South
♠ J 9
♥ A J 9 8 7 6 2
♦ A K 4
♣ 4

West leads the ♠10, his partner's ♠Q winning as you follow with the card you are known to hold, the ♠J. East switches to the ♦J. How do you play?

Here, to avoid a ruff, we use the stratagem of prematurely removing the entry to the danger hand, i.e. the defender due to lead the suit that will be ruffed. You are up against a very well-judged line of defence by East on this hand.

You appear to have an easy nine tricks with five trumps, three top diamonds, and the ♣A. But East is obviously angling for a diamond ruff, available if the suit breaks 5-2 or worse. If East himself is short of diamonds, you can simply strip him of trumps by playing ace and another (East can hardly have more than two trumps on this auction). But it is more likely that East is aiming for a ruff in his partner's hand. In that case, if you start on trumps immediately, West may win and play a second diamond, intending to put his partner in with the ♠A for a ruff after winning his second trump trick. To disrupt the order of play, you must win the diamond and play a spade yourself at once. After that, you have time to draw trumps.

North
♠ K 8 4 2
♥ 10
♦ Q 8 3
♣ A 7 6 3 2

West
♠ 10 3
♥ K Q 5 4 3
♦ 7 2
♣ J 9 8 5

East
♠ A Q 7 6 5
♥ —
♦ J 10 9 6 5
♣ K Q 10

South
♠ J 9
♥ A J 9 8 7 6 2
♦ A K 4
♣ 4

Points to remember

1. Note that West's double is dubious for two reasons: poor intermediate trumps and lack of outside tricks.
2. Try to anticipate the order of the defence and look for ways to disrupt it where possible.

We now turn to kitchenware to cut defenders adrift.

Scissors are an important tool

The Scissors Coup can be used to cut defenders' communications —
this is often applicable in a suit contract when a ruff is threatened.

Dealer South				**North**
Neither vulnerable				♠ K 10 9
W	**N**	**E**	**S**	♥ Q 9 8 5
			1♣	♦ J 7
1♥	1NT	2♥	3♦	♣ Q J 6 5
pass	4♣	pass	5♣	

South

♠ A Q

♥ 3

♦ A Q 10 9

♣ K 10 9 8 7 4

How do you play on the lead of the ♦2?

The lead must surely be a singleton and you can see that, if West has
the ♣A, he will win an early trump, and put his partner in with a
heart honour to receive a diamond ruff. How can you avoid this
when lack of entries precludes an early heart discard on a spade?
The solution is to hope that West has the ♠J and trade a heart loser
to East for a spade loser to West. Win the lead and cash the ♠A.
Overtake the ♠Q with the ♠K and lead the ♠10, intending to discard
your singleton heart. West wins and you are out of danger.

North

♠ K 10 9

♥ Q 9 8 5

♦ J 7

♣ Q J 6 5

West

♠ J 6 4 2

♥ K J 10 4 2

♦ 2

♣ A 3 2

East

♠ 8 7 5 3

♥ A 7 6

♦ K 8 6 5 4 3

♣ —

South

♠ A Q

♥ 3

♦ A Q 10 9

♣ K 10 9 8 7 4

Note that, if the ♠J is among three or more with East, you never had a chance anyway.

Points to remember

1. Understand the rationale of the bidding and line of defence. West would hardly have led round to your bid suit without good reason.

2. Where communications are vital to defenders, be on the lookout for ways to cut them off. This kind of loser-on-loser situation (more on that later) crops up frequently but is often overlooked.

Let them have their bit of fun!

Most of the time as declarer, you will attempt to prevent your opponents from getting a ruff. Nevertheless, there are occasions when the best policy is to allow the threatened ruff to materialise. Tricks may be saved elsewhere. On this next hand, your generosity in the ruffing area will be repaid.

Dealer West
Neither vulnerable

W	N	E	S
pass	1♣	1♥	1♠
pass	2♠	pass	4♠

North
♠ 6 5 2
♥ 10 4 2
♦ A 7
♣ A K J 5 3

South
♠ A J 10 9 8 7
♥ K
♦ Q 2
♣ Q 7 4 2

West leads the ♥8 to his partner's ♥A and East returns the ♣8, all too obviously a singleton. You win in dummy and play a trump, East playing low. Do you finesse or rise?

In cases like this, consider the consequences of going *wrong*. The contract is in danger if South plays his ace, and East has both trump honours and West the ♦K. South needs to cash his long club for a diamond discard but East can interrupt twice with high trumps, first knocking out dummy's ♦A and then cashing the ♦K.

   Contrast this with the position where South finesses and West produces a trump honour. A club ruff follows but then, even if East can attack diamonds safely, South wins, draws the outstand-

ing trump and cashes the clubs, discarding the diamond loser. The
contract is made for the loss of two trumps and the ♥A.

North
♠ 6 5 2
♥ 10 4 2
♦ A 7
♣ A K J 5 3

West
♠ 3
♥ 9 8 6
♦ K 8 6 5 4 3
♣ 10 9 6

East
♠ K Q 4
♥ A Q J 7 5 3
♦ J 10 9
♣ 8

South
♠ A J 10 9 8 7
♥ K
♦ Q 2
♣ Q 7 4 2

Points to remember

1.   Mentally run through the two variations and consider the consequences
     of taking the wrong view.
2.   Note that East does no better to switch to diamonds at trick two. He gets
     a diamond trick but gives up the chance of a club ruff. Now South
     takes the percentage line of two trump finesses and concedes one trick
     in each non-club suit.

To draw or not to draw?

Now consider this next, more complex example which illustrates a
similar theme:

Dealer North
E-W vulnerable

W	N	E	S
	pass	pass	1♣
pass	3♣		

North
♠ K 3 2
♥ 8 7
♦ A 10 4 3
♣ A 6 5 2

South
♠ Q 9 4
♥ J 3
♦ K J 9 5
♣ K Q 10 9

West cashes two top hearts and switches to the obviously single-ton ♦Q. You win and play two top trumps, East following with the ♣J and discarding a diamond on the second round. How do you continue?

The problem here is that, if you draw the remaining trumps, you will not be able to establish a spade trick without allowing the de-fenders to cash countless hearts. Against that, if you fail to draw trumps, preferring to knock out the ♠A first, you will suffer a ruff and be in danger of losing two spade tricks in addition to the two hearts for five in all and defeat.

The approach again is to consider the position of the ♠A. Suppose it is with West: then you can play a small spade from hand. If West rises, there is no ruff and, if he doesn't, you can win in dummy, draw the remaining trumps and claim nine tricks. But the critical case arises when the ♠A is with East. Now, if you play a small card towards dummy, East will capture dummy's ♠K, give his partner a diamond ruff, and you will still have another spade to lose for one down.

So try taking two rounds of trumps, ending in dummy, and playing a low spade towards your hand. Now East is stuck. If he rises and gives his partner a diamond ruff, he will forgo the second spade trick. If he ducks, you win and draw trumps, claiming nine tricks as before. Finally, if you start with a low spade from dummy and West has the ♠A after all, again no harm is done; you lose two spade tricks but no ruff.

Points to remember
1. Note the manner in which the two possible lines of play were considered in regard to the position of the ♠A.
2. With these appalling splits in the minors, it is true that East-West are cold for 3♥ but that is no reason to mess up your contract of 3♣!

Trump Technique

7

Use and Misuse of Trumps

In life, we learn that it is unwise to spend money purely for the sake of it — later on it may not be there when needed! However, it can be even more stupid not to spend it when it ought to be used. A similar truism applies to the use of trumps.

Enjoy the free drink!

Try for the ruff when it can only gain and cannot cost.

Dealer North				North
Neither vulnerable				♠ Q 9 6 4
W	**N**	**E**	**S**	♥ 3 2
	pass	pass	2♣	♦ Q 8 5 4
2♠	pass	pass	6♥	♣ 8 7 5

South
♠ 5
♥ A K Q 9 8 7 5 4
♦ —
♣ A K Q 2

West leads the ♠A, East playing the ♠8, and switches to the ♥10, East following with the ♥J. How do you play from here?

There will be no problem if the clubs are 3-3, but, if they are 4-2, you will need to ruff one, precluding another round of trumps. You must hope that, if the clubs are indeed 4-2 or worse, the hand with the short clubs is also out of trumps. Play three rounds of clubs. If they break, the hand is over; if not, you may get a ruff anyway:

North
♠ Q 9 6 4
♥ 3 2
♦ Q 8 5 4
♣ 8 7 5

West
♠ A K J 10 7 3
♥ 10
♦ A K 10 6
♣ 6 4

East
♠ 8 2
♥ J 6
♦ J 9 7 3 2
♣ J 10 9 3

South
♠ 5
♥ A K Q 9 8 7 5 4
♦ —
♣ A K Q 2

Points to remember

1. If the clubs are indeed 3-3, nothing is lost by playing that suit before touching trumps.

2. Note East's play of the ♠8 on trick one, trying to give his partner the necessary information in that suit — the count.

Test the water!

Sometimes a side-suit needs to be tested *before* completing the drawing of trumps because a ruff may be needed:

Dealer South
N-S vulnerable

W	N	E	S
			1♥
pass	2♣	pass	2♦
pass	2♠[1]	pass	4♦
pass	6♦		

[1] fourth suit, game-forcing

North
♠ K 4 3
♥ 8 3
♦ A 9 6
♣ A J 9 7 5

South
♠ A
♥ A K Q 7 5
♦ K J 10 8 3
♣ 8 2

West leads the ♣6. How do you play?

The club loser can easily be avoided by discarding it on the ♠K but there is still a possible trump loser and the hearts need to be established. The order of play is important. If the hearts are 3-3, there is no problem and there is no danger in playing the suit before touching trumps. But, if they are 4-2, a ruff in dummy will be needed and this is most safely taken after exactly two rounds of trumps are drawn.

On winning the club, you should cash the ♠A and ♥A. Now cross to dummy with the ♦A, take the club discard on the ♠K and lead a second heart towards your hand. If East has a singleton heart, he will simply be ruffing a loser with a trump trick which is probably his anyway. On winning the second heart, cash a second top trump and ruff a low heart in dummy, eventually conceding the ♦Q (if she hasn't already fallen on the first two rounds of trumps).

	North	
	♠ K 4 3	
	♥ 8 3	
	♦ A 9 6	
	♣ A J 9 7 5	
West		**East**
♠ Q 10 9 7		♠ J 8 6 5 2
♥ 10 9 4 2		♥ J 6
♦ Q 5 4		♦ 7 2
♣ 6 4		♣ K Q 10 3
	South	
	♠ A	
	♥ A K Q 7 5	
	♦ K J 10 8 3	
	♣ 8 2	

Points to remember

1. Note that the second round of hearts was played starting from dummy to protect against East's holding a singleton. Ideally, both the first and second rounds should be played from dummy in case East is void, but entries, as here, may be at a premium.

2. Note that testing hearts before trumps are drawn can never cost. If there is a really bad break, typically with West having the shortage, there are losers anyway and the contract could never be made by drawing trumps in order to avoid defensive ruffs and overruffs.

The honours can wait!

Having seen the idea, try this next example.

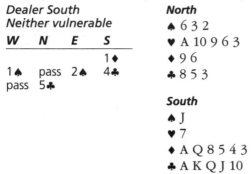

Dealer South
Neither vulnerable

W	N	E	S
			1♦
1♠	pass	2♠	4♣
pass	5♣		

North
♠ 6 3 2
♥ A 10 9 6 3
♦ 9 6
♣ 8 5 3

South
♠ J
♥ 7
♦ A Q 8 5 4 3
♣ A K Q J 10

West starts with two top spades and you notice partner has shown a great deal of faith in your bidding. How do you continue?

Clearly the diamond suit will have to be brought in and that may well require a ruff in dummy. You should, therefore, not play more than one round of trumps before crossing to the ♥A and taking the diamond finesse. If that loses, you ruff the next major card, draw one more round of trumps, cash the ♦A and ruff a diamond in dummy, hoping that the ♣9 is with the long diamonds. Now draw trumps and claim the rest.

North
♠ 6 3 2
♥ A 10 9 6 3
♦ 9 6
♣ 8 5 3

West
♠ A K 10 8 4
♥ Q J 2
♦ K 7
♣ 6 4 2

East
♠ Q 9 7 5
♥ K 8 5 4
♦ J 10 2
♣ 9 7

South
♠ J
♥ 7
♦ A Q 8 5 4 3
♣ A K Q J 10

Observe the effect if you draw two rounds of trumps early. Now, if the diamond finesse loses and West has a third trump, he will play

it and then, with dummy exhausted of trumps, you will be deprived
of your diamond ruff.

Points to remember

1.   Note the bidding of North, putting full trust in his partner who bid to the
     four-level alone. The ruffing value and ♥A are likely to be useful. Alter
     the hand by replacing the ♥A with the ♥K and ♥Q; that is one point
     more but the case for bidding 5♣ is now reduced markedly. Admittedly,
     partner could be 0-2-6-5 but his actual hand is more likely.
2.   Note the timing of drawing trumps to leave just enough trump cards
     in dummy to ensure the ruff, which will be needed if the diamond finesse
     fails.

Swing high! Swing low!

When taking ruffs in dummy, the order can often be critical. If you
are threatened with an overruff, consider ruffing high first time to
hold the lead and keep dummy's trump holding intact.

Dealer West   **North**
N-S vulnerable   ♠ Q 10 4 2

W	N	E	S	♥ A 9
3♦	pass	pass	3♥	♦ A
pass	4♥			♣ Q 8 6 5 3 2

                         South
                         ♠ A 8
                         ♥ K Q 10 8 7 6
                         ♦ 7 6 4 3
                         ♣ A

West leads the ♦Q; East drops the ♦K. Plan the play.

If the trumps break 3-2, hardly guaranteed on this auction, there
are nine tricks and a chance of a tenth if you guess the spade position correctly. But a better line is to try for two diamond ruffs in
dummy. The snag now is that, if you ruff the first diamond with the
♥9, East may overruff and his trump return will not only deny you
a second ruff but also leave you no hope of a second spade trick.

   Therefore, you should play to ensure two ruffs by crossing to the
♣A and ruffing a diamond with the ♥A! Return to hand with a club,

ruffed by the ♥K (to prevent an overruff and trump switch) and only now ruff a diamond with the ♥9. If East overruffs, that could well be with a trick which was his anyway; you now have seven trump tricks and three aces to total ten for your contract. If East fails to overruff, you can give up the ♥J later, if necessary.

North
♠ Q 10 4 2
♥ A 9
♦ A
♣ Q 8 6 5 3 2

West
♠ 7 6 3
♥ 2
♦ Q J 10 9 8 5 2
♣ J 9

East
♠ K J 9 5
♥ J 5 4 3
♦ K
♣ K 10 7 4

South
♠ A 8
♥ K Q 10 8 7 6
♦ 7 6 4 3
♣ A

Points to remember

1. Pre-emptive bidding constitutes a warning of bad breaks in all suits. This should be borne in mind in both bidding and play. As illustration here, it is a well-known tip that, when a pre-empter leads the suit he has bid, that is an indication of a singleton or void trump. The rationale behind this is that, with longer trumps, typically in a 7-3-2-1 shape, he will often lead a short suit in attempt to set up a ruff for himself.

2. Note the technique of the early high ruff to avoid an overruff and ensure an extra ruffing opportunity.

8

Coping with Enemy Ruffs

Ruffing, of course, is not the sole privilege of declarer. The defenders will be keen to use their trumps to best advantage and we must consider how to minimise their pleasure. Declarer has a number of possible counters.

Trade your waste!

Where trump losers are inevitable, consider playing a side-suit early for discards, noting that, if defenders ruff, it may be that they are winning a trick which was theirs anyway.

				North
Dealer East				♠ A K 8 7 6
E-W vulnerable				♥ 6 5 3
W	**N**	**E**	**S**	♦ 8 7
		pass	1♥	♣ Q 8 7
pass	1♠	pass	2♣	
pass	3♥	pass	4♥	**South**
				♠ J
				♥ J 10 9 4 2
				♦ A 3 2
				♣ A K J 2

West leads the ♦J. How do you play?

After South's optimism in going on to game, there seems little to be done to avoid three trump losers and a diamond and declarer will need a bit of luck. Suppose the trumps are 3-2, with the doubleton consisting of honours, and the clubs are 3-3. Now four rounds of clubs will put the defenders on the spot:

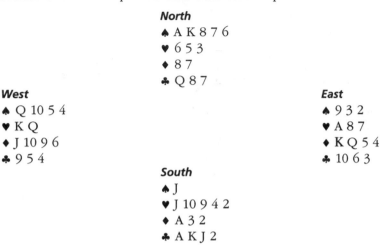

North
♠ A K 8 7 6
♥ 6 5 3
♦ 8 7
♣ Q 8 7

West
♠ Q 10 5 4
♥ K Q
♦ J 10 9 6
♣ 9 5 4

East
♠ 9 3 2
♥ A 8 7
♦ K Q 5 4
♣ 10 6 3

South
♠ J
♥ J 10 9 4 2
♦ A 3 2
♣ A K J 2

On the fourth round, you will discard a losing diamond and, regardless which defender ruffs, it will be with a trick which was theirs anyway. All you will lose are the three trump tricks. Admittedly, this line may result in two down if a defender ruffs with a low trump from a doubleton or singleton and holds two or fewer clubs but it's a small price to pay for the only chance of making the contract. In any case, the odds favour the long trumps being with the short clubs so you might well break even anyway.

Points to remember

1. After some optimistic bidding (South should probably pass 3♥, having been warned that his partner's high cards are likely to be in the wrong suit), you are in a poor contract so you must assume that cards lie favourably for you and play accordingly.

2. Look for possibilities for early discards of losers in this manner. Usually, at worst, you will break even.

We now turn to situations where declarer has to face the inevitable but can minimise the amount of spilt milk.

Salvage the maximum from the wreckage!

If a ruff is threatened, look for ways to cut your losses. Try the following example.

Dealer North
E-W vulnerable

W	N	E	S
	pass	1♦	1NT
pass	2♦[1]	dbl[2]	2♥[3]
pass	4♥		

[1] transfer to hearts
[2] good diamonds
[3] good hearts

North
♠ Q 3
♥ J 10 9 7 3
♦ 5 2
♣ K Q J 2

South
♠ A 4 2
♥ A K Q 2
♦ K 6 4 3
♣ 8 3

West leads the ♦J to his partner's ♦A; East returns the ♦7. How do you play from here?

This hand seems a simple matter of winning the second diamond, drawing trumps and conceding a spade and a club quietly. One down! As long as you realise the likelihood of the ♦K being ruffed, you will play low at trick two, intending to discard dummy's spade loser after trumps have been drawn. Effectively, what you are doing is trading a spade loser for a diamond loser, gaining a trick because your diamond winner has been kept intact.

North
♠ Q 3
♥ J 10 9 7 3
♦ 5 2
♣ K Q J 2

West
♠ K 8 7 6 5
♥ 8 6 4
♦ J
♣ 10 6 5 4

East
♠ J 10 9
♥ 5
♦ A Q 10 9 8 7
♣ A 9 7

South
♠ A 4 2
♥ A K Q 2
♦ K 6 4 3
♣ 8 3

Points to remember
1. Note East's return of his lowest diamond, indicating a desire for the return of the lower-ranking suit (clubs) after the ruff; a spade from West would be fatal for the defenders.
2. Look for similar situations where a ruff is threatened; if it costs nothing to hold your winner until later, think twice before playing it prior to trumps being drawn.

Don't begrudge the occasional crash!

Having seen the idea, can you spot the correct line on this next example? It may help to remember that sometimes one has to be cruel to be kind.

Dealer West
Neither vulnerable

W	N	E	S
3♦	dbl	pass	4♥

North
♠ A Q 10 2
♥ Q 10 8 3
♦ K 4 3
♣ A 10

South
♠ K
♥ K J 9 7 4
♦ 10 7
♣ Q 8 4 3 2

West leads the ♣7. How do you play?

This could well be a singleton and, in any case, the ♣K is likely to be with East so there is little to be gained and much to be lost by playing low from dummy. More importantly, even, a diamond ruff is threatened since East surely has only one. So you win with the ♣A and then what?

Drawing trumps immediately still risks a diamond to the ♦A and a ruff. So you should attack spades first. With the club entry prematurely removed from dummy, you will not be able to cash all three spade tricks so it is best to start with the ♠A, crashing your ♠K, and then follow with the ♠Q, discarding a diamond, so that you are in a position to overruff East on the second round of that suit. After the two spades, you can draw trumps, hoping to restrict your losses to a trump, the club and the ♦A, or try a cross-ruff given the quality of your heart spots.

North
♠ A Q 10 2
♥ Q 10 8 3
♦ K 4 3
♣ A 10

West
♠ J 9
♥ 6 2
♦ A Q 9 8 6 5 2
♣ 7 5

East
♠ 8 7 6 5 4 3
♥ A 5
♦ J
♣ K J 9 6

South
♠ K
♥ K J 9 7 4
♦ 10 7
♣ Q 8 4 3 2

Note that, as the cards lie, you will drop the ♠J and can now go on to play the ♠10 discarding your other diamond. If West ruffs low, you have broken even (having traded a diamond loser for a second trump loser) but, if West has a trump void or singleton ace, you gain an overtrick.

Points to remember
1.   Note the reasons for rising with the ♣A at trick one.
2.   Observe that crashing your ♠K is unlikely to cost.

9

Trump Control

It is usual to choose as trumps a suit where declarer and dummy between them own a majority. In the play, it is usually vital to ensure that the position stays that way! Few things in life give a worse impression than flaunting wealth. At the bridge table, it can be fatal.

Showing off is a mug's game!

Be reluctant to ruff in the long hand without good reason. It always saddens me to see quite experienced players taking infinite pleasure in scoring ruffs in their own hand when all they are doing is shortening their own trumps, losing control, and winning tricks which would have been theirs later anyway. Here is a straightforward example.

Dealer East
E-W vulnerable

W	N	E	S
		pass	2♣
pass	3♣	pass	3♠
pass	4♠	pass	5♠
pass	6♠		

North
♠ K 5 3
♥ 7 5 3 2
♦ 5
♣ A 8 5 3 2

South
♠ A 10 9 6 2
♥ A K Q
♦ A K 9 7 3
♣ —

How do you play on the lead of the ♣Q?

Realistically, you will have to ruff two diamonds in dummy and hope to limit your trump losers to one. Win the first club, discarding the ♦3, and cross to hand in diamonds, ruffing the second round. Enter your hand with a heart and ruff another diamond. Now cash the ♠K and return to hand again in hearts to continue to draw trumps.

North
♠ K 5 3
♥ 7 5 3 2
♦ 5
♣ A 8 5 3 2

West
♠ Q
♥ 9 8 6 4
♦ Q 8 4
♣ Q J 10 6 4

East
♠ J 8 7 4
♥ J 10
♦ J 10 6 2
♣ K 9 7

South
♠ A 10 9 6 2
♥ A K Q
♦ A K 9 7 3
♣ —

Note that, if you cross to hand by ruffing a club, you will shorten your trumps to the same length as East's and lose control. On winning the third trump, East will force you by playing another club; now he will have more trumps than you do and cannot be denied a second trick.

Points to remember

1. Ruffing in the long trump hand when you aren't forced to can be costly. It should only be done in the following circumstances:

    a) you are planning a dummy reversal, i.e. treating declarer's hand as dummy.

    b) you are deliberately trying to shorten your trumps to execute a trump coup.

    c) you have no other safe or convenient entry to hand and plenty of trumps so that shortening yourself will not jeopardise control.

    d) you have a number of very low trumps in hand and few in dummy and the only way to score them, before they are drawn by opponents, is to take early ruffs in hand.

    e) it is necessary to establish a long suit in dummy.

f) you have plenty of trumps and need to eliminate or at least partially eliminate a side-suit prior to an endplay.

g) you have plenty of trumps and are trying to get a count on a side-suit.

2. The above hand falls into none of these categories. There is nothing to be gained by ruffing a club in hand.

Lock the door before the horse bolts!

Where the opponents have a degree of trump control, you need to arrange for them to blow their trumpet at the proper time. If trump tricks need to be lost, arrange to lose them while you are still in control. This situation is likely to apply when there is a choice of plays in trump suit. This is an illustrative example.

Dealer West
E-W vulnerable

W	N	E	S
pass	1♣	pass	1♥
pass	3♣	pass	3♥
pass	4♥		

North
♠ 3 2
♥ K 9
♦ A 7 5
♣ A K Q 9 8 4

South
♠ 10 8 7 6
♥ A J 10 7 5 4
♦ Q
♣ J 5

How do you play on the lead of the ♦J?

There will be no problem if you pick up the trumps without loss as you will then have six trump tricks, at least four clubs, and a diamond. But, if you fail to locate the ♥Q, there could be trouble. As indicated earlier, the way to tackle this type of problem is mentally to try out all the possible lines and visualise what might happen if you misguess. The ♦K is likely to be with East on the lead, so you should win the first diamond; you now have three options::

1) bang down the two top trumps and switch to clubs if the ♥Q fails to appear. Defenders are likely to ruff the third round of clubs (if not earlier) and cash three spades — one down.

2) cash the ♥K and take a finesse through East; defenders may cash three or more spade tricks — one down.

3) run the ♥9 immediately; if it loses, defenders can only cash two spade tricks, as the ♥K polices the third round.

North
- ♠ 3 2
- ♥ K 9
- ♦ A 7 5
- ♣ A K Q 9 8 4

West
- ♠ K J 9
- ♥ Q 3 2
- ♦ J 10 9 6 2
- ♣ 10 2

East
- ♠ A Q 5 4
- ♥ 8 6
- ♦ K 8 4 3
- ♣ 7 6 3

South
- ♠ 10 8 7 6
- ♥ A J 10 7 5 4
- ♦ Q
- ♣ J 5

Points to remember

1. This kind of situation often arises when dummy is short both in trumps and in a weak side-suit.
2. The first-round finesse only sacrifices the chance of picking up a singleton ♥Q — a small price to pay for ensuring the contract, even at pairs.

Keep your armour on as long as possible!

Dealer East
E-W vulnerable

W	N	E	S
		1♣	1♥
3♣	3♦	pass	3♠
pass	4♥		

North
- ♠ 3
- ♥ 7 2
- ♦ A Q 7 6 3 2
- ♣ 10 9 6 5

South
- ♠ Q 10 9 6 4
- ♥ A K 10 9 5 4
- ♦ K 5
- ♣ —

West leads the ♣Q. How do you play the hand?

Clearly the diamonds will have to break for you to have any chance. But if you merely bang down three rounds of trumps, defenders would then be in a position to take three spade tricks if the ♠J is with

West. You must arrange to lose the trump trick while dummy can
still police a spade attack, i.e. on the first round. After ruffing the first
trick, you should play a low trump from your hand.

North
- ♠ 3
- ♥ 7 2
- ♦ A Q 7 6 3 2
- ♣ 10 9 6 5

West
- ♠ A J 7
- ♥ Q 8 3
- ♦ 9 4
- ♣ Q J 7 3 2

East
- ♠ K 8 5 2
- ♥ J 6
- ♦ J 10 8
- ♣ A K 8 4

South
- ♠ Q 10 9 6 4
- ♥ A K 10 9 5 4
- ♦ K 5
- ♣ —

Defenders win this trick but cannot hurt you in spades and you
take eleven tricks for the loss of just one trump trick and a spade.

Points to remember

1.   Note again the 'short trumps, short side-suit' position in the dummy.
2.   Losing the first trump trick costs nothing except in the case where they
     are breaking 4-1 with the singleton being an honour.

Unselfishness is the safe way!

Dealer East
E-W vulnerable

W	N	E	S
			1♠
pass	2♦	pass	2♠
pass	4♣[1]	pass	4♥
pass	5♠	pass	6♠

[1] splinter, in support of
    spades

North
- ♠ A 8 7
- ♥ Q 10 8 6
- ♦ A K Q 10 4
- ♣ 7

South
- ♠ K Q 9 6 5
- ♥ A 9
- ♦ J 9
- ♣ A 9 8 2

Here is another example where declarer must beware of a poor
trump split. West leads the ♣Q. How do you play?

If the trumps break 3-2, you have twelve tricks on top and can easily make an overtrick by adding a club ruff in dummy at trick two. But what if trumps are 4-1? All of a sudden, the contract is in danger.

Try a few lines. If you draw three rounds of trumps early and play on diamonds, the long trump hand will probably ruff in at an early stage and cash club winners. Taking two rounds of trumps and, if a defender shows out, starting on diamonds may not work either: they may ruff in and play a club, forcing dummy to ruff. The diamonds are now dead and you are left two tricks short, restricted to six trump tricks, two top diamonds, the ♣A and the ♥A. Cashing the ♠A and then ducking a trump is better but still not good enough. Now, if they play clubs, you can ruff and claim. But, if they return trumps, you are left a trick short.

The correct line is to win the first club and duck a trump trick immediately. Now the defence has no answer. If they play a club, you ruff, cash the ♠A, cross to hand with the ♥A, draw trumps and claim. If they play a trump, the ♠A wins and a heart to the ♥A follows. Now ruff a club, return to hand in diamonds, draw trumps and claim. If they return a diamond, win in hand, ruff a club, cash the ♠A, return to the ♥A, draw trumps and cash the remaining diamonds.

It will pay to study each of these variations on detail.

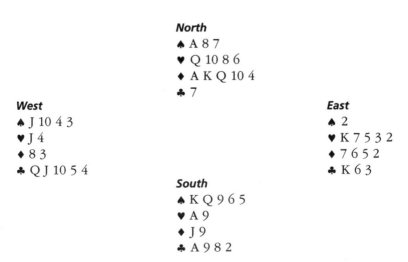

```
                        North
                        ♠ A 8 7
                        ♥ Q 10 8 6
                        ♦ A K Q 10 4
                        ♣ 7
West                                            East
♠ J 10 4 3                                      ♠ 2
♥ J 4                                           ♥ K 7 5 3 2
♦ 8 3                                           ♦ 7 6 5 2
♣ Q J 10 5 4                                    ♣ K 6 3
                        South
                        ♠ K Q 9 6 5
                        ♥ A 9
                        ♦ J 9
                        ♣ A 9 8 2
```

Points to remember

1. Note the early loss of the trump trick to maintain control.
2. Also observe the use of entries in each variation.
3. It remains to discuss whether one should play like this at pairs, where the sacrifice of the overtrick could be costly in terms of matchpoints. This is debatable and a good case can be made for the safety play. In anything but a top-class field, a good proportion of the pairs will not have bid the slam and therefore making it is already likely to be well above average. If you judge that the field is strong and that most people will be in it, the case in favour of ignoring the safety play is much stronger.

Crossruff at the proper time!

It is a well-known dictum that one needs to cash side-suit winners early before starting a cross-ruff; we shall see some examples later. Not so well-known, however, is the need to play the correct number of rounds of trumps first. Usually, the correct number is zero, but there are exceptions, notably where there is the danger of unwelcome overruffs.

Dealer West
E-W vulnerable

W	N	E	S
pass	pass	pass	2NT
pass	3♣[1]	pass	3♥
pass	4♥		

[1] Stayman

North
♠ 10 6 3 2
♥ 7 5 4 2
♦ 8 6
♣ K J 3

South
♠ A K
♥ A 8 6 3
♦ A 7 5 3
♣ A Q 5

West leads the ♦Q. How should you play?

With a certain diamond loser, you will need the trumps to split 3-2 and you will have to crossruff diamonds and spades. But, to ensure that the doubleton trump does not interfere with the crossruff, you need to play exactly two early rounds of trumps. That implies losing the first round and winning the second round so that you, rather than the defenders, are on play after two rounds. A similar consideration applies to diamonds. One early trick must be lost and it is best to duck the first round and win the second before ducking a trump. After winning any return, you cash the trump ace and the club winners and cross-ruff the rest, allowing the defenders to take their outstanding trump whenever the mood takes them.

North
♠ 10 6 3 2
♥ 7 5 4 2
♦ 8 6
♣ K J 3

West
♠ 9 7 5
♥ K Q 10
♦ Q J 10 4
♣ 9 6 4

East
♠ Q J 8 4
♥ J 9
♦ K 9 2
♣ 10 8 7 2

South
♠ A K
♥ A 8 6 3
♦ A 7 5 3
♣ A Q 5

Points to remember

1.   Note the early duck in diamonds. Winning trick one and returning the suit may not be good enough: they could play a third round and then a fourth when in with the first round of trumps. That could lead to an overruff by the doubleton-trump hand and defeat.

2.   Similarly note the duck of the first round of trumps — ace and another might allow defenders to play a third round, ruining the crossruff.

10

Some Standard Techniques

Earlier, I advised against ruffing in hand for the sake of it. Nevertheless, on occasions, there may be good reason. One of the most potent pointers towards a dummy reversal is a 4-3 fit in a side-suit. Here is a simple example.

Four-three — look back at me!

Dealer East
E-W vulnerable

W	N	E	S
		pass	1♣
pass	2♦[1]	pass	2♥
pass	3♦	pass	3♠
pass	4♥	pass	4NT
pass	5♦[2]	pass	5NT[3]
pass	6♣		

[1] forcing club raise
[2] 1 or 4 key cards
[3] asking for anything extra

North
♠ 8 5 3
♥ A Q 10
♦ A Q 7
♣ A K 10 7

South
♠ A Q 10 6
♥ K J 9 5
♦ 5
♣ Q J 9 4

How do you play on the lead of the ♦J?

First of all, there is nothing to be gained by taking the diamond finesse (which is likely to be wrong) with a singleton in hand: there is nothing useful to be discarded. So you should win the first trick.

After that, it seems a simple matter of drawing trumps and taking two spade finesses for a 75% chance of success. But it is a pity to go down when they both fail, as in the lay-out below. Here you are unlucky enough to find a 4-1 trump split, too. Thus you will also fail if you try the following line: draw trumps, play four rounds of hearts, discarding a spade and take one spade finesse. If it loses, hope to drop the other honour by ruffing. In any case, this plan offers a lower chance of success than the two finesses.

North
♠ 8 5 3
♥ A Q 10
♦ A Q 7
♣ A K 10 7

West
♠ K J 9 2
♥ 7 6 4 3
♦ J 10 9 4
♣ 6

East
♠ 7 4
♥ 8 2
♦ K 8 6 3 2
♣ 8 5 3 2

South
♠ A Q 10 6
♥ K J 9 5
♦ 5
♣ Q J 9 4

The contract is cold, however, and it is easy to see if only you consider the South hand as 'dummy'. At trick two, ruff a diamond in hand, return to dummy with a trump and ruff dummy's last diamond. Now cash the last high trump in hand, return to dummy in hearts and draw the remaining trumps to claim the contract with six trump tricks, four hearts and the aces of diamonds and spades.

If the trumps break 3-2, you can even try the spade finesse for an overtrick. Here, you should refrain from doing so as you will be defeated if West has the ♠K and a fourth diamond. Even at pairs, you are probably already on a good score having bid and made the slam, so I should recommend settling for the twelve tricks.

Points to remember

1. It is natural to treat declarer's hand as 'master' and to find ways for dummy to look after declarer's losers. Often it pays to turn the tables.

2)   When playing a dummy reversal, the same rule applies as for taking early ruffs in dummy: refrain from drawing trumps until the ruffing process is completed.

Having seen the idea, you can try this next one.

Chiefs are not exempted from doing the work!

Dealer East				North
E-W vulnerable				♠ Q 7 2
W	**N**	**E**	**S**	♥ J 10 9
		pass	1♥	♦ A K 5
pass	2♣	pass	2♠	♣ A 7 5 4
pass	3♦	pass	3♥	
pass	5♥[1]	pass	5♠[2]	**South**
pass	7♥			♠ A K 8 4

[1] asks about trump quality
[2] grand slam try with
excellent trumps

South
♠ A K 8 4
♥ A K Q 7 5
♦ 9 6 2
♣ 8

North has grossly overestimated his trick-taking potential here, but South is not entirely devoid of blame for the auction. In any event, the final contract is, to put it kindly, highly optimistic. Still, you are there now, and you have to make the best of it. How do you play this hand on the lead of the ♦Q?

There are eleven tricks on top and the spades will have to be 3-3 for a twelfth.   Ruffing a diamond in dummy is out of the question as this would allow only two rounds of trumps to be drawn. The fourth round of spades, on which dummy's losing diamond would be discarded, would then surely be ruffed. The solution is to turn the hand upside down and ruff three clubs in hand.

Win the lead in dummy, cash the ♣A, and ruff a club high. Return to dummy with a low trump to the ♥J and ruff another club high. Another trump to dummy's ♥10 is followed by a further high club ruff. Now a diamond to the ♦K is followed by drawing the last enemy trump, and the spades are cashed for thirteen tricks — six trumps, four spades, two diamonds and the ♣A.

North
♠ Q 7 2
♥ J 10 9
♦ A K 5
♣ A 7 5 4

West
♠ 6 5 3
♥ 6 4 3
♦ Q J 10
♣ K J 10 9

East
♠ J 10 9
♥ 8 2
♦ 8 7 4 3
♣ Q 6 3 2

South
♠ A K 8 4
♥ A K Q 7 5
♦ 9 6 2
♣ 8

Points to remember

1. Dummy reversal is often suggested when it is impossible to discard dummy's losers (to prepare for a ruff in dummy) without the defenders' interrupting.

2. Good trumps in dummy, usually a trebleton, which are capable of drawing trumps, are needed — usually but not always. Sometimes, when top trump losers are inevitable, poor trumps will serve as well, as in the next example:

Little things mean a lot!

Dealer East
E-W vulnerable

W	N	E	S
		pass	1♥
pass	1♠	pass	2♣
pass	2♦[1]	pass	2NT
pass	4♥		

[1] fourth suit, game-forcing

North
♠ A 7 6 2
♥ 8 4 3
♦ K J 10
♣ K 8 6

South
♠ 8
♥ A 7 6 5 2
♦ A Q 8
♣ A 5 4 2

West finds a good trump lead — the ♥J. You allow this to hold, East following with the ♥9, and he continues with the ♥10 to your ♥A and West's ♥Q. How do you play from here?

You could try three rounds of clubs at once, hoping either for a 3-3 break or that the short-club hand has the last trump — certainly a good chance. But why enjoy a 'good' chance when the contract is a certainty on a dummy reversal? Just play the ♠A and ruff a spade, cross to dummy twice more with diamonds and take two more spade ruffs. Then cash your remaining minor-suit winners for ten tricks.

North
♠ A 7 6 2
♥ 8 4 3
♦ K J 10
♣ K 8 6

West
♠ K 10 9 4 3
♥ J 10
♦ 9 7 6 2
♣ 10 7

East
♠ Q J 5
♥ K Q 9
♦ 5 4 3
♣ Q J 9 3

South
♠ 8
♥ A 7 6 5 2
♦ A Q 8
♣ A 5 4 2

Note that, even if the diamonds break very badly and defenders ruff in early, they are ruffing with a natural trump trick. They cannot now draw any more trumps and the most you can lose is a club and two trumps.

Points to remember

1. Note that the dummy reversal is effective in situations where the number of trumps in declarer's hand is reduced to less than that of dummy.
2. Note the duck of the first round of trumps. If South wins, he is defeated if the defender with the doubleton is able to interrupt the dummy reversal process, either by ruffing diamonds or overruffing in spades — admittedly unlikely, but why take such an unnecessary risk?

Let's move on now to look at some more positions where we are going to ruff in both hands.

Clear the track before running on it!

When planning a cross-ruff, cash your top side winners first.

Dealer West
Both vulnerable

W	N	E	S
pass	1♣	1♦	1♥
2♦	4♦¹	pass	4♥
pass	6♥		

¹ heart support, no
   diamond losers

North
♠ A 10 8 6
♥ A Q J 10
♦ —
♣ A Q J 10 2

South
♠ K 2
♥ 9 8 7 6 5 2
♦ Q J 3 2
♣ 3

How do you play on the lead of the ♦7?

Watch three 'top-class' players in action:

'Expert 1' ruffed the lead, crossed to the ♠K and played a trump, rising with the ♥A when West showed out. Now came the ♣A, a club ruff, diamond ruff, club ruff, diamond ruff, club ruff, on which East discarded his second spade, and the ♠A, ruffed by East who cashed the trump king and a top diamond for two down.

'Expert 2' realised that all the trumps in dummy were needed to ruff losing diamonds and did so, using the ♠K and club ruffs as entries. But he failed to cash the ♠A which was ruffed by East. The king of trumps had to be lost as well; one down.

Expert number three simply cashed his two top spades and ♣A and cross-ruffed the rest of the hand; there was now no defence.

North
♠ A 10 8 6
♥ A Q J 10
♦ —
♣ A Q J 10 2

West
♠ Q 7 5 4 3
♥ —
♦ 7 6 5 4
♣ K 8 6 5

East
♠ J 9
♥ K 4 3
♦ A K 10 9 8
♣ 9 7 4

South
♠ K 2
♥ 9 8 7 6 5 2
♦ Q J 3 2
♣ 3

Points to remember

1. Note the need of all four of dummy's trumps to ruff losing diamonds. Even if the ♥A were to drop a singleton ♥K, you would, at best, break even.

2. Did you comment on that opening lead? Bidding like that cries out for a trump lead and yet West failed to produce one, strongly suggesting a void. The first declarer showed a lack of awareness in this respect.

3. Note that failure to cash winners before the crossruff may allow a defender to strip himself of the appropriate suit while the crossruff is in progress. Now your winners are likely to be ruffed. This next example is similar to one which proved crucial in an international match with the world championship at stake.

If you have no ready cash, arrange it in time!

Dealer West
Both vulnerable

W	N	E	S
3♦	dbl	pass	5♥
pass	6♥		

North
♠ Q 8 5 4 3
♥ A K Q 9
♦ —
♣ Q 10 4 3

South
♠ A K
♥ J 10 8 7
♦ Q 5 4 3 2
♣ K 2

Some optimistic bidding has landed you in a dubious slam. How do you play this contract on the lead of the ♦A?

A 3-3 spade split is unlikely on the bidding. Furthermore, even if it happens, a 3-2 trump split as well is even less likely, given that West has a very long diamond suit and the three spades already credited to him. Even assuming both suits behave, drawing trumps and cashing spades will give you eleven tricks only. A crossruff is a better chance, but some preparatory work is needed.

Ruff the opening lead and play a club towards the ♣K. If it holds, cash the top spades, cross to dummy with a diamond ruff and cash the third top spade, discarding the losing club. If that

holds, cross-ruff the rest of the hand (all the trumps are high) for a
club, three spades and eight trump tricks. Note that a trump lead
would have ruled out this line.

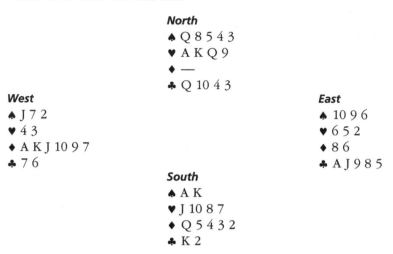

North
♠ Q 8 5 4 3
♥ A K Q 9
♦ —
♣ Q 10 4 3

West
♠ J 7 2
♥ 4 3
♦ A K J 10 9 7
♣ 7 6

East
♠ 10 9 6
♥ 6 5 2
♦ 8 6
♣ A J 9 8 5

South
♠ A K
♥ J 10 8 7
♦ Q 5 4 3 2
♣ K 2

This was how the successful declarer played. Observe the difference
in events in the other room where the declarer, after the same lead,
was so obsessed with getting diamond ruffs that he used his spade
entries for that purpose. The play went: ♦A ruffed, ♠A, diamond
ruff, ♠K, diamond ruff on which East discarded his last spade. That
ruled out cashing the ♠Q and declarer was left a trick short. His
team never recovered from the loss — world championship to the
defenders.

Points to remember

1. Often, as here, side winners may have to be established, typically by
   knocking out an ace, so they can be cashed before the crossruff starts.
2. In this connection, it is instructive to consider what happens if East rises
   with the ♣A and switches to a trump. He ruins the crossruff but is now
   allowing declarer two club tricks instead of one. Replay the hand:

1) ♦A ruffed	5) ♠A	9) ♣Q	13) trump
2) club to East's ♣A	6) ♠K	10) ♠Q	
3) trump	7) trump	11) ♠8	
4) ♣K	8) trump	12) ♠5	

   and the contract is still made.
3. An initial trump lead defeats the slam.

Finally, we look at positions in which declarer can save himself by coalescing his losers.

Two wrongs CAN make a right!

Throw a loser on a loser to win! Look for situations where you can set up extra winners by this technique.

Dealer South
Neither vulnerable

W	N	E	S
			2♣
pass	2♦[1]	pass	3♠[2]
pass	4♥	pass	6♠

[1] negative
[2] solid suit, demanding a cue bid from North

North
♠ 10 8
♥ A 8
♦ Q J 10 6
♣ 10 9 6 4 2

South
♠ A K Q J 9 6 4 2
♥ Q J 6 4
♦ A
♣ —

How do you play after West finds the one lead to give you problems, a trump, East following?

You have ten top tricks and can establish an eleventh in hearts. But, irrespective of how you play those hearts, you can't guarantee a twelfth: try it. Suppose you play the ♥A and then low towards hand; West could win and, if he has the outstanding trump, he will play it to leave you a trick short. Alternatively, running the ♥Q could lose to East and now, if he has the outstanding trump, you again will be left with an inescapable heart loser.

You must thus ignore hearts and take advantage of dummy's diamonds. Win the first spade, cash the ♦A and return to dummy in trumps. Now run the ♦Q, discarding a heart. If it loses to West, you have twelve tricks. If East covers, ruff, and try the heart finesse for an overtrick, later returning, if necessary, to the ♥A to cash the other two diamonds.

Points to remember

1)   Note that this loser-on-loser play is effective, regardless of the position of the ♦K.

2)   Also note the heart position and that, although you can guarantee the contract if you know the position of the ♥K, there is no play to cater for both situations.

Let the lady time her appearance!

Here is another example involving ruffing in dummy

Dealer West				**North**
Neither vulnerable				♠ 7 6
W	**N**	**E**	**S**	♥ A 4
pass	1♣	pass	2♠	♦ A 4
pass	3♣	pass	3♥	♣ A 9 8 5 4 3 2
pass	3 NT	pass	4♠	
pass	5♦	pass	6♠	**South**
				♠ A K Q J 10 2
				♥ K J 10 6
				♦ 6 2
				♣ 7

How do you play on the lead of the ♦5?

There are ten obvious top tricks and an eleventh easily establishable in hearts. But there are two ways of playing the heart suit and a danger of losing a heart and a diamond.

Again, the loser-on-loser technique gives the best chance for the contract. Win the first diamond and play ♥A, ♥K, and ♥J. If the ♥Q does not appear from West, discard dummy's losing diamond. If East wins, South's second diamond can be ruffed in dummy. If the ♥J is covered, dummy ruffs and, provided there is no overruff, South can afford to draw trumps and give up a diamond. Only in the cases where West has five or more hearts to the queen and East can overruff dummy, or East has four or more hearts to the queen, will the contract fail. In the second case, East will play a fourth heart and West, if he holds either the ♠8 or ♠9, can ruff higher than dummy.

Points to remember

1.   You should have at least considered the possibility of setting up the clubs but noted that the early removal of the ♦A leaves dummy short of the required entries. On a trump lead, declarer must go for the clubs, using the two aces as entries and hoping for a 3-2 club split.

2.   Note that it is premature to draw even one round of trumps. If the ♥Q is then lost to East, a second round of trumps leaves dummy without a trump to take the crucial ruff.

Nothing is sacred!

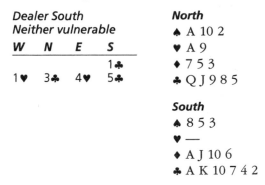

Dealer South
Neither vulnerable

W	N	E	S
			1♣
1♥	3♣	4♥	5♣

North
♠ A 10 2
♥ A 9
♦ 7 5 3
♣ Q J 9 8 5

South
♠ 8 5 3
♥ —
♦ A J 10 6
♣ A K 10 7 4 2

Finally, consider this hand. How do you play this contract on the lead of the ♥K? Most important — do not rush!

Hasty play to trick one will ruin many a declarer. Here we are going to use the loser-on-loser technique to avoid losing a trick to a dangerous defender. It seems incredible that, with the ♥A facing a void, a trick should be lost in the suit but that is the only way to be certain to make the contract!

You can see that, provided East has either diamond honour, two finesses will keep your losses to a diamond and a spade; but what if they are both with West? Now you must draw trumps and eliminate the majors before leading a low card to the ♦10 to leave West on play. He will then have to give you either a free finesse in the suit or a ruff and discard.

You can also see that, unless West has three spade honours, you will at some stage have to lose a trick in that suit to East. Now an early diamond from him (while West still has an exit card) will bring about your downfall. But try the effect of ducking the ♥K, discarding a low spade from hand. Win the next trick (probably a spade switch), take one round of trumps and discard your remaining low spade on the ♥A. Ruff a spade in hand, return to dummy in trumps and ruff the last spade from dummy in hand. Return again to dummy in trumps and play a diamond to the ♦10, losing to West. West is now endplayed, forced to give you a ruff and discard or a free diamond finesse.

North
♠ A 10 2
♥ A 9
♦ 7 5 3
♣ Q J 9 8 5

West
♠ Q 9 7 4
♥ K Q 10 5 4
♦ K Q 8
♣ 6

East
♠ K J 6
♥ J 8 7 6 3 2
♦ 9 4 2
♣ 3

South
♠ 8 5 3
♥ —
♦ A J 10 6
♣ A K 10 7 4 2

Points to remember

1) Note that you could only draw one round of trumps early. As they broke 1-1, that was sufficient. But even if they had been 2-0, you need trumps as entries to dummy in the later play and, if you draw two rounds early, the South hand runs out of trumps, spoiling the ruff-and-discard position.

2) Look out for positions like the hearts above where you can a refuse a trick that the non-dangerous defender will win, and avoid a dangerous loser in another suit. These come up more often than many players realise.

Conclusion

We have reached the end of what I hope has been a reasonable cross-section of common situations in which average club declarers continually go astray. An assimilation of at least a proportion of them will make you a far more formidable opponent and much sought-after partner!